Family Storytime

Twenty-Four Creative Programs for All Ages

ROB REID

AMERICAN LIBRARY ASSOCIATION
Chicago and London
1999

Project editor: Joan A. Grygel

Cover and text design by Todd Sanders.

Composition by The Publishing Services Group in New Aster using
QuarkXpress 3.3 on a Macintosh platform.

Printed on 50-pound offset opaque, a pH-neutral stock, and bound in
10-point coated cover stock by Data Reproductions Corporation

The paper used in this publication meets the minimum requirements
of American National Standard for Information Sciences—Permanence
of Paper for Printed Library Materials, ANSI Z39.48-1992. ∞

Library of Congress Cataloging-in-Publication Data

Reid, Rob
    Family storytime : twenty-four creative programs for all ages /
by Rob Reid.
    p.   cm.
    Includes bibliographical references and index.
    ISBN 0-8389-0751-2 (alk. paper)
    1. Storytelling—United States.   2. Children's libraries—Activity
programs—United States.   3. Libraries—Services to families—United
States.   I. Title.
    Z718.3 .R45 1999
    027.62'51—dc21   98-40765

Printed in the United States of America.

03 02 01 00 99   5 4 3 2 1

4831

To Aunt Jean—
Whom I hold dear in my heart

Contents

Acknowledgments   vii

Introduction   1

What about Those Teens?   2
How to Use This Book   3
Openings and Closings   4
Other Tips for a Successful Family Storytime   6

The Programs   9

2nd-Generation Favorites   11
Altered Endings & Twisted Tales   19
Barnyard Fun   28
Big & Gray   36
Birdland   46
Black Bears, Brown Bears, Polar, Panda, & Teddy
    Bears   55
Bubbly Bubble Bathtime   62
Creepy Crawlers   69
Frogs, Snakes, Turtles, 'Gators, & Crocs   77
Jammy Jamboree   87

Meow & Squeak!   95

Mouthsounds   104

The Name Game   113

Outrageous Hats & Sensible Shoes   123

Papas, Granddads, & Uncles   131

Super Moms (& Super Grandmas & Super Aunts)   139

The Tricksters   147

Uh-Oh! Accidents!   158

Under the Deep Blue Sea, Sea, Sea   166

What'cha Gonna Wear?   174

What's Cooking?   182

Wild Critters   191

Winter Wonderland   199

Woof & Wag   207

One Final Round of Applause   215

Bibliography of Picture Books and Poems   217

Discography of Songs and Tunes   235

Index of Titles   241

Acknowledgments

I'd like to thank the following librarians and performers who have helped shape my storytelling and writing over the years. They are each and every one very special to me.

Sonia Ackerman
Shu Cheng
Kate Fitzgerald-Fleck
Colleen Hannafin
Miriam Hansen
Linda Madlung
Julie Majkowski
Roxanne Neat
Bruce O'Brien
Sue Richardson
Sandy Robbers
David Stoeri
Kathleen Thomson
Kris Adams Wendt
Marge Loch-Wouters

And of course, thanks to my family for sitting in on and performing in countless Family Storytime sessions—Jayne, Laura, Julia, Alice, and Sam.

"Alligator Stomp" and "Five Froggies" copyright 1994 Anna Moo™ from Anna Moo Crackers. Good Moo's Productions, GOODMOOS@CCGNV.NET. 352-472-6223.

"The Little Duckling" and "Three Little Snowmen" permission granted by the author, Elizabeth Vollrath.

"My Brother Eats Bugs" by Hans Mayer and Frank Gosar. Myther Music/Silly Business. P.O. Box 1674, La Crosse, WI 54602-1674.

"The Night the Froggies Flew" by Colleen and Uncle Squaty. North Side Music, 1314 Birch Street, Eau Claire, WI 54703. 800-828-9046.

"Owl Moon" words and music copyright Bruce O'Brien. 604 Newton Street, Eau Claire, WI 54701, found on his recording *Love Is In the Middle*, distributed by Tomorrow River Music. Inspired by the book *Owl Moon*, copyright 1987 by Jane Yolen. Used by permission of Curtis Brown, LTD. All rights reserved.

"Put Your Thumb in the Air" by Joe Scruggs and Dee Gibson from the recording *Deep in the Jungle* by Joe Scruggs. Copyright 1987 Educational Graphics Press, Inc. Shadow Play Records, P.O. Box 180476, Austin, TX 78718. 800-274-8804.

"Porridge" from *The Three Bears Rhyme Book* by Jane Yolen. ©1987 Harcourt Brace & Company.

"We Will Read Books" permission granted by the author, Julie Majkowski.

Introduction

Parents were not encouraged to attend story programs when I first began my career as a children's librarian. Now, I wouldn't think of presenting a story program without them.

Family Storytimes are essential to public libraries today. When parents and caregivers are present, the enjoyment and educational aspects of the story program are heightened. The adults become positive role models for the children for reading, reading-readiness activities, and becoming life-long library users. Adults learn proper techniques for reading aloud. They learn stories, fingerplays, songs, and activities. They remember stories, songs, and fingerplays from their own childhood and are thrilled to learn new ones. They may not admit it, but adults also enjoy being read to.

Some librarians may be intimidated by the presence of adults or older children in a story program. Hopefully, they'll give it a try and realize the advantages of an all-age program. Margaret Read MacDonald, in her books *Bookplay: 101 Creative Themes to Share with Young Children* and *Booksharing: 101 Programs to Use with Preschoolers*, advocates encouraging adults to attend story programs for the following reasons:

1. Adults can lend a helping hand during storytime. They can help with more-intricate activities and crafts or simply snuggle with the children for longer stories. They become the librarian's accomplices, not adversaries.

2. Parents have a chance to interact with other parents before and after the program. They receive social and intellectual stimulation.

3. Story activities will more likely be continued outside the library.
4. Children see their parents or caregivers in playful, creative roles.
5. Your audience is doubled.

Personally, I find Family Storytimes to be the most enjoyable of all library programs to conduct for a number of reasons: There is a wider range of material from which to choose. Good material that may not work in a Preschool Storytime may work with great success in a Family Storytime setting. For example, I would never dream of performing a spoonerism story, reading a chapter from a Gary Paulsen memoir, or telling a long joke like "The Klunge Maker" for a Preschool Storytime. Yet, they are all included in this book. When adults are present, this type of story and activity goes over well, even for the younger set. I also find myself performing the same material on multiple levels. The children may laugh or express astonishment at one point in the story, while the adults react to other parts. There is that unmeasurable satisfaction of looking at the audience and seeing children wrapped up in the arms of their parents or grandparents, all with smiles on their faces.

What about Those Teens?

Teens and preadolescents are important members of the family, too, and we shouldn't assume they're not interested in Family Storytimes. Needless to say, they usually won't attend without encouragement. I find a typical Family Storytime audience to be made up of one-third adults, one-third preschoolers, and one-third elementary-age children. The teens will attend, but it usually takes a little incentive from the librarian. For example, invite the teens to help present the program. Reach them through literature, drama, or early childhood classes. When I take the time to look, I always find teens who are more than ready to perform in some capacity for an audience. We also have teenagers who regularly ask if they can volunteer at the library. Assign them to help with Family Storytime. Some secondary classes require students to fulfill a certain number of community volunteer hours. Sign them up for Family Storytime. Have the teens act out poetry, participate in reader's theater, manipulate a puppet, or read one of the picture books. Their parents will attend the program to watch them, and they'll bring younger siblings and other family members with them.

Don't overlook the senior citizens in your community. Again, if you get them involved as participants in the program, their families will follow and give them support. The seniors, like the teens, usually won't attend unless someone makes that little effort to attract them. Once they come, the seniors will also be glad to read a book, recite a poem, or hold a puppet.

How to Use This Book

One way to keep families returning is to prepare highly participative programs. Included here are two dozen programs that have met great success. They all contain a good mixture of picture books, poetry, music, and movement activities. Much of the material is used in my regular Preschool Storytimes. Other material is more likely to be unique to the multigenerational program. While most of the programs have been designed for a solid, 30-minute program, others have been loaded a little longer. Rearrange the lesson plan to fit your style. Each chapter contains lists of alternate material that fits the theme. The "Mix and Match" Section in each program recognizes librarians' personal tastes and the holdings of different libraries. The lists include supplementary picture books, poems, songs and musical activities, fingerplays and movement activities, videos, and other resources.

The twenty-four programs reflect traditional story themes, such as those on bears, dogs, and clothing, as well as unorthodox themes on topics from accidents and mouthsounds to names and tricksters. Each chapter opens with a "Program at a Glance" for quick reference and to help you locate and organize materials. The symbols key for this section is as follows:

chapter book

picture book (or story)

craft

poem

draw and tell

reader's theater

felt story

riddle

fingerplay

string story

movement activity

video

music (musical activity or song)

The "Preparation and Presentation" sections go into great detail about practicing and presenting the material. I conduct a lot of story program workshops around the country and get several requests from workshop participants on presentation techniques. In this book, I also comment how a certain book or activity might be received differently by an audience of mixed ages as opposed to an age-specific group, such as Preschool Storytime. With some of the material in the lesson plans, I simply provide short annotations.

Openings and Closings

I usually find or develop a different ritual opening for each program. These are not listed within the various lesson plans. In the past, I have used a variety of poems, songs, or chants ranging from Shel Silverstein's poem "Invitation," from his book *Where the Sidewalk Ends,* to several "Hello" songs found listed in my book *Children's Jukebox: A Subject Guide to Musical Recordings and Programming Ideas for Songsters Ages One to Twelve,* published by the American Library Association.

I have also used the traditional activity "Criss-Cross Applesauce," which works especially well for family programs. Have the children turn their backs to their parents. The parents should perform the following actions on each child. Once the activity is finished, have the children switch places with the adults and let the youngsters perform the actions.

Criss-Cross Applesauce

Criss-cross
> *(Make an* X *on the child's back)*

Applesauce,
> *(Tap each shoulder)*

Spiders crawling up your back,
> *(Walk fingers up the child's back)*

Cool breeze,
> *(Blow gently on child's neck)*

Tight squeeze,
> *(Give the child a hug)*

Now you've got the shivers.
> *(Give the child a light tickle)*

I have also written a little opening ditty that works well, especially for the teens and adults:

Some of These Stories

Some of these stories you've heard before,
Some of them will be quite new.
Rest assured that EVERY word is
Absolutely,
Positively,
GUARANTEED
to be (almost) true!

I have also closed my various story programs over the years with a variety of ritual "Goodbye" songs. These are also listed in *Children's Jukebox*. Now, however, I close every program with my "Wave Goodbye" rap, which has also been published as a picture book by Lee and Low Books.

Wave Goodbye

Wave high,
Wave low,
I think it's time,
We gotta go.
Wave your elbows,
Wave your toes,
Wave your tongue
And wave your nose.
Wave your knees,
Wave your lips,
Blow a kiss
With fingertips.
Wave your ears,
Wave your hair,
Wave your belly
And derriere.
Wave your chin,
Wave your eye,
Wave your hand
And say goodbye.

Other Tips for a Successful Family Storytime

Adults can lend a helping hand to develop proper audience behavior. Many people today (adults as well as children) are used to talking right over television and videos and find it hard to sit quietly for a 30- to 40-minute program. Some find it hard to settle back down after you have led them in a highly participative activity. Set the tone before a program begins.

With the help of several colleagues, we have fashioned a "preshow" statement. Here is a sample:

> Children, put on your best listening skills. That means sit still and be quiet unless I ask you to talk or move around. Parents, feel free to take any children who are restless or noisy out to the hallway until they are ready to rejoin us. I appreciate your cooperation and consideration for the other audience members and myself. Thank you.

It's amazing how well this statement works. When I don't say it, I usually have to deal with inappropriate behavior and parents who aren't sure what to do when their children misbehave. When I do remember to make the statement, it seems as if I have "given permission" for the adults to help out.

I liken Family Storytimes to family reunions. Many families have busy schedules and are hard pressed to have time together. Schedule Family Storytimes evenings and weekends when most family members can attend. Remember that the term *family* is used in a broader sense than it was a few decades ago. Families include single-parent families, stepfamilies, grandparents as the primary caregivers, and other instances as well as the traditional nuclear family. Remember this as you advertise this event.

If presenting a Family Storytime is a new experience for you, I hope you will find it very rewarding. If you have been presenting multigenerational programs for a long time, I hope you will find new material or techniques to help you prepare and present a very satisfying and important type of library program.

The Programs

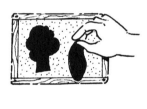

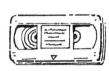

.

2nd-Generation Favorites

Program at a Glance

MOVEMENT ACTIVITY	"Hands on Shoulders"
PICTURE BOOK	*Make Way for Ducklings* by Robert McCloskey
PICTURE BOOK	*Millions of Cats* by Wanda Gag
FINGERPLAY	"Where Is Thumbkin?" from *One, Two, Three, Four, Live!* by Sharon, Lois and Bram
MUSIC	"The Skunk Song" from *Wee Sing Silly Songs*
PICTURE BOOK	*A Fish Out of Water* by Helen Palmer
MUSIC	"On Top of Spaghetti" by Tom Glazer from *Shake It All About* by Little Richard
MUSICAL ACTIVITY	"The Hokey Pokey" by Charles P. Macak, Larry Laprise, and Tafft Baker from *1-2-3 for Kids* by The Chenille Sisters
PICTURE BOOK	*Goodnight Moon* by Margaret Wise Brown
MUSIC	"Be Kind to Your Parents" by Harold Rome from *Make Believe* by Linda Arnold

Preparation and Presentation

For both the publicity and program introduction, mention that all of the stories and songs in this program are stories and songs that "your parents" (and maybe their parents and their parents before them) heard "when they were your age."

 ## "Hands on Shoulders"
traditional

This activity works as a good icebreaker for an intergenerational program. Ask the parents how many of them did "Hands on Shoulders" when *they* went to storytime. Have everyone stand and act out the commands.

> Hands on shoulders, hands on knees,
> Hands behind you if you please;
> Touch your shoulders, now your nose,
> Now your hair and now your toes;
> Hands up high in the air,
> Down at your sides and touch your hair,
> Hands up high as before,
> Now clap your hands,
> One, two, three, four.

 ### *Make Way for Ducklings*
Robert McCloskey

This is a long story for the very young, but they usually sit still when they hear about the ducklings Jack, Kack, Lack, Mack, Nack, Ouack, and Pack.

 ### *Millions of Cats*
Wanda Gag

Tell this wonderful story with or without the book. The pictures are fascinating, but tiny for a large group to see. Get the audience involved by teaching them the refrain "Cats here / Cats there / Cats and kittens everywhere / Hundreds of cats /

Thousands of cats / Millions and Billions and Trillions of cats." For added fun, ask the audience to make "Millions and Billions and Trillions of meows."

"Where Is Thumbkin?"
traditional

Here is another fingerplay that has been popular for generations.

> Where is Thumbkin? Where is Thumbkin?
> > *(Hold up both thumbs. Have thumbs interact with each other.)*
> Here I am. Here I am.
> How are you today, sir? Very well, I thank you.
> Run away, run away.
> > *(Hide thumbs behind back)*
>
> > *(Repeat for Pointer, Tall Man, Ring Man, and Pinkie)*

"The Skunk Song"
traditional

Here is one I remember singing a lot when I was a child. For maximum effect, use a skunk puppet to sing the skunk's lines and lift its tail at the end of the song. Cue your audience to say "PU!" The song can be easily recited instead of sung.

> I stuck my head in a little skunk's hole
> And the little skunk said "Well, bless my soul,
> Take it out! Take it out! Remove it!"
>
> I didn't take it out and the little skunk said
> "If you don't take it out, you'll wish you had.
> Take it out! Take it out! Remove it!"
> P-U! I removed it!

A Fish Out of Water
Helen Palmer

Before I start reading this funny book about a boy who over-feeds his goldfish, I ask the audience if anyone knows which famous author was married to Helen Palmer. Since it's rare to find someone who knows the answer, I give them a hint. I tell them her married name was Geisel. Perhaps one or two parents know by now. If no one has guessed, I tell them that Mr. Geisel wrote under the name Dr. Seuss. "Helen Palmer was married to Dr. Seuss and she wrote one of my favorite books when I was a little boy."

"On Top of Spaghetti"
Tom Glazer

This hilarious adaptation of "On Top of Old Smokey" is as popular today as it was when written by Glazer more than 30 years ago. In fact, today's young generation is probably more familiar with this parody than with the original folk song. I sing it a cappella and many kids and parents join me for the first few verses. The song can be found on Glazer's recording *Children's Greatest Hits* and Little Richard's recording *Shake It All About*.

"The Hokey Pokey"
Charles P. Macak, Larry Laprise, and Tafft Baker

Get everyone on their feet for the musical activity "The Hokey Pokey." If there is anyone on the planet who doesn't already know this popular dance, then they'll learn it in a matter of seconds. As corny as it is, it's still a lot of fun, especially with a roomful of kids and adults. It can be found on several recordings including *1-2-3 for Kids* by The Chenille Sisters, *Kidding Around* by Greg and Steve, and Little Richard's *Shake It All About*.

Goodnight Moon
Margaret Wise Brown

Wind down the session with a reading of the classic *Goodnight Moon*. After the reading, have the audience say goodnight to the various objects in the library. "Goodnight, books. Goodnight, shelves. Goodnight, computers. Goodnight, librarians."

"Be Kind to Your Parents"
Harold Rome

Finish the program with a heartfelt rendition of the 1945 hit, "Be Kind to Your Parents." The song ends with the wonderful phrase "Someday you may wake up and find you're a parent, too." I usually sing this a cappella, but you can also play the song from either the recording *Make Believe* by Linda Arnold or *Pure Imagination* by Michael Feinstein.

Mix and Match

ADDITIONAL PICTURE BOOKS

Brown, Marcia. *Stone Soup.*

>Three hungry soldiers come to town and immediately show the selfish villagers how to make a feast out of water and stones.

Burton, Virginia. *Mike Mulligan and His Steam Shovel.*

>Mike and his steam shovel Mary Anne prove they are still worthy of great work.

Krasilovsky, Phyllis. *The Man Who Didn't Wash His Dishes.*

>A man decides to leave the dirty dishes until the next night . . . and the next night . . . and so on until he has to use the ash trays, vases, even the soap dish for his utensils.

Leaf, Munro. *The Story of Ferdinand.*

>Ferdinand the bull prefers smelling flowers to fighting matadors.

Minarik, Else Holmelund. *A Kiss for Little Bear.*

>A kiss gets passed from animal to animal before it reaches its final destination.

ADDITIONAL POEMS

"Halfway Down" by A. A. Milne from *Read-Aloud Rhymes for the Very Young,* edited by Jack Prelutsky.

"I Eat My Peas with Honey" from *A New Treasury of Children's Poetry,* edited by Joanna Cole.

"If We Didn't Have Birthdays" by Dr. Seuss from *The Random House Book of Poetry for Children,* edited by Jack Prelutsky.

"The People Upstairs" by Ogden Nash from *The Random House Book of Poetry for Children,* edited by Jack Prelutsky.

"The Purple Cow" by Gelett Burgess from *A New Treasury of Children's Poetry,* edited by Joanna Cole.

ADDITIONAL SONGS AND MUSICAL ACTIVITIES

"I Know an Old Lady Who Swallowed a Fly" by Peter, Paul and Mary from *Peter, Paul and Mommy, Too.*

"If You're Happy and You Know It" by Little Richard from *Shake It All About.*

"Here We Go Loop 'D Loo" by Greg and Steve from *We All Live Together, Vol. 1.*

"Put Your Finger in the Air" by Woody Guthrie from *Woody's 20 Grow Big Songs.*

"She'll Be Comin' Round the Mountain" by Little Richard from *Shake It All About.*

ADDITIONAL FINGERPLAYS AND MOVEMENT ACTIVITIES

"Open Them, Shut Them"
traditional

> *(Act out all motions with hands)*
> Open them, shut them,
> Open them, shut them,
> Give a little clap.

Open them, shut them,
Open them, shut them,
Fold them in your lap.

Creep them, creep them,
Creep them, creep them,
To your rosy cheek.
Open wide your shiny eyes
And through your fingers peek.

Open them, shut them,
Open them, shut them.
To your shoulders fly.
Let them, let them,
Like little birds,
Flutter to the sky.

Falling, falling,
Slowly falling,
Nearly to the ground,
Quickly raise your little fingers
Twirl them all around.

Open them, shut them,
Open them, shut them,
Give a little clap.
Open them. shut them,
Open them, shut them,
Fold them in your lap.

"I'm a Little Teapot"
traditional

I'm a little teapot, short and stout,
Here is my handle,
(Place hand on hip)
Here is my spout.
(Hold other arm out sideways)
When I get all steamed up, then I shout,
Tip me over and pour me out.
(Bend sideways toward extended arm)

VIDEOS

Make Way for Ducklings. Weston Woods. (11 min.)

Mike Mulligan and His Steam Shovel. Weston Woods. (11 min.)

Stone Soup. Weston Woods. (10 min.)

Altered Endings & Twisted Tales

Program at a Glance

POEM
"Old Mother Hubbard" from *The New Adventures of Mother Goose* by Bruce Lansky

PICTURE BOOK
The Three Little Wolves and the Big Bad Pig by Eugene Trivizas

MUSICAL ACTIVITY
"A Trio of Myopic Rodents" adapted by Rob Reid

PICTURE BOOK
"Letter from Goldilocks" from *The Jolly Postman and Other People's Letters* by Janet and Allen Ahlberg

PICTURE BOOK
Somebody and the Three Blairs by Marilyn Tolhurst

MUSICAL ACTIVITY
"Hickory Dickory Dock" adapted from *Wee Sing*

PICTURE BOOK
"Letter from Red Riding Hood" from *The Jolly Postman and Other People's Letters* by Janet and Allen Ahlberg

MUSICAL ACTIVITY
"Little Rap Riding Hood" from *Crazy Gibberish* by Naomi Baltuck

PICTURE BOOK
"The Hungry Wolf" from *Yo! Hungry Wolf* by David Vozar

READER'S THEATER
"Dincerella" adapted by Rob Reid

MUSICAL ACTIVITY
"The New Wheels on the Bus" adapted by Rob Reid

POEM
"Star Light, Star Bright" from *The New Adventures of Mother Goose* by Bruce Lansky

Preparation and Presentation

A "Fractured Fairy Tales" type of theme is perfect for a mixed-age audience. Most of the stories, songs, and verse contain many levels of humor. The children will enjoy the basic plot changes and general silliness, while the teens and adults will appreciate the subtleties.

"Old Mother Hubbard"
Bruce Lansky

This fractured version has the dog ordering a pizza after seeing the bare cupboards. Tell your audience that this is a sample of things to come as "we take a new look at old favorites."

The Three Little Wolves and the Big Bad Pig
Eugene Trivizas

The big bad pig makes life miserable for the three soft and cuddly wolves. The adults will laugh at the description of the wolves' concrete house (complete with a video entrance phone) while the children will enjoy the action. All ages will feel satisfied when the pig sees the error of his ways and dances the tarantella.

"A Trio of Myopic Rodents"
adapted by Rob Reid

Here is a new version of "Three Blind Mice" that also works on several levels of humor. The adults will enjoy the new phrasings while the children will enjoy the nonsensical sounds. (The tune can be found on *Wee Sing Silly Songs*.)

> A trio of myopic rodents, a trio of myopic rodents,
> Observe how they perambulate, observe how they
>   perambulate,
> They all circumnavigated the agriculturalist's spouse,
> She excised their extremities with a kitchen utensil,
> Did you ever observe such an occurrence in your
>   existence,
> As a trio of myopic rodents, a trio of myopic rodents.

Ask the adults and the older children to suggest new ways to recite well-known nursery rhymes. An example to get them started is "Jack and Jill ascended an elevation to retrieve a canister of moisture." Since it's hard to come up with this type of clever activity on the spot, ask the audience to be thinking of one. If they think of one at home, ask them to write it down, bring it in, and post it somewhere in the library for all to see.

"Letter from Goldilocks"
Janet and Allen Ahlberg

The Jolly Postman and Other People's Letters is a collection of letters from one fairy tale character to another. Most of the letters in this book are too detailed to share all at once in a story program. Share a few select letters one by one throughout the program. In her letter, Goldilocks writes an apology to the bears and tells them that her father will fix the chair.

Somebody and the Three Blairs
Marilyn Tolhurst

This Goldilocks reversal story shows a little bear sneaking into the Blair family's house while they are out for a walk. The loudest laughs will come when you read Baby Blair's lines, such as "Issa big teddy bear," with an "itty bitty baby" voice.

"Hickory Dickory Dock"
traditional, adapted by the Wee Sing Company

By now, everyone's ready for a stretching activity and this version of "Hickory Dickory Dock" fits the bill. Ask everyone to stand tall and turn themselves into a grandfather clock. One of their hands can be a mouse. Starting at their feet, the "mouse" travels up the entire length of the "clock." Act out the motions for the new verses found on the recording, such as "The clock struck two, the mouse said 'Boo' / The clock struck three, the mouse said 'Wheee!' / The clock struck four, the mouse said 'No more!' "

"Letter from Red Riding Hood"
Janet and Allen Ahlberg

In this excerpt from *The Jolly Postman and Other People's Letters* Red's lawyers from the firm Meeny, Miny, Mo, and Company, send the wolf a letter warning him to stop harassing Grandma. The lawyers also mention that the Three Little Pigs have decided to sue for damages.

"Little Rap Riding Hood"
Naomi Baltuck

Don your dark glasses and a red scarf and perform the hottest, "baddest" rap version of "Little Red Riding Hood" ever created. If memorizing the rap is too challenging, purchase Baltuck's recording of the same title and lip-sync to this fast-paced, tongue-twistin' rap.

"The Hungry Wolf"
David Vozar

While you're in the rapping mood, check out this story of "The Three Little Pigs" written in rap verse.

"Dincerella"
Rob Reid

I love to write spoonerisms. Spoonerisms are crowd favorites. The older listeners enjoy the creative wordplay while the youngsters think the whole thing just sounds silly. A spoonerism is created when you switch parts of words. Ask four volunteers from the audience or line up four teens ahead of time to read my version of "Dincerella." Warn them to read the script very slowly.

READER 1:   Once a time upon, Dincerella lived with her sticked wepmother and her sad misters, who kept her as beezy as a biz.

READER 2:   She had to poke the sots and dipe the wishes.

READER 3:   She had to steep the sweps and flop the moor.

READER 4:	She had to bake the meds and bust the dunks.
ALL:	Everything had to look spac and spin.
READER 1:	But grid she dumble?
ALL:	No!
READER 2:	She kept a liff upper stip.
READER 3:	She kept her grind to the nosestone.
READER 4:	She knew that's the way the crumble cookies.
READER 1:	The sticked wepmother and the sad misters bent to a wall given by some ditch rude.
READER 2:	Dincerella was mad she got left behind, and she blarted to stubber.
READER 3:	Who should appear but her merry god fom.
READER 4:	She made some dancy fuds for Dincerella to bear to the wall.
ALL:	Do you know how Dincerella bent to the wall?
READER 1:	It wasn't in a vini-man.
READER 2:	It wasn't in a dull bozer.
READER 3:	It wasn't in a trickup puck (with fancy flood maps).
READER 4:	It wasn't even in a trump duck.
ALL:	She went in a bandsome huggy made from a pig bumpkin.
READER 1:	At the ball, Dincerella woogie-boogied with the ditch rude.
READER 2:	Never one to spot the hoglight, she dashed out at the moke of stridnight.
READER 3:	The ditch rude told his men to keep their peels eyed for the girl.
READER 4:	He told them . . .
READER 1:	"If the woo fits, share it."
READER 2:	They tried to sit the flipper on the sad misters' finky steet.
READER 3:	Dincerella said . . .

READER 4:   "Hey! Slop that flipper on my fainty deet!"

ALL: The flipper sit!

READER 1:   Wick as a quink, the two were wappily harried.

READER 2:   As for the sticked wepmother

READER 3:   And the sad misters, they learned that

READER 4:   The eek shall inherit the mirth.

Several nonspoonerism "fractured" reader's theater scripts can be found in the book *Frantic Frogs and Other Frankly Fractured Folktales for Reader's Theatre* by Anthony D. Fredericks.

"The New Wheels on the Bus"
adapted by Rob Reid

Everyone knows the traditional "Wheels on the Bus." (The tune can be found on *The Elephant Show Record* by Sharon, Lois and Bram.) Here's my take-off . . .

Let's get off the bus and get into a nice red shiny
     SPORTS CAR!
The wheels on the sports car go
     "Roundroundroundroundround . . ."
The horn on the car goes "Meep meep meep meep . . ."
The motor on the car goes "rrrrrrRRRRRRRRRRRrrrrrr"

Now let's get out of the car and get into a ROCKET SHIP!
The boosters on the rocket go "Whoossshhhh . . ."
The radio on the rocket goes "Garble squawk garble . . ."
The people on the rocket go "Hey! I'm floating! . . ."

Let's get off the rocket and get into something more
     exciting . . . A DONKEY CART!
The wheels on the cart go "Klippity Klop . . ."
The driver on the cart goes "Giddyup . . ."
The donkey on the cart goes "Hee-haw . . ."
The kids, moms, and dads go "That's all!"

"Star Light, Star Bright"
Bruce Lansky

This hilarious take on the classic nighttime rhyme has the child praying to stay dry all night.

Mix and Match

ADDITIONAL PICTURE BOOKS

Ada, Alma Flor. *Dear Peter Rabbit.*

> Here's another fun exchange of letters featuring several storybook characters.

Calmenson, Stephanie. *The Principal's New Clothes.*

> A vain principal is persuaded to wear an invisible suit in this spoof of the Hans Christian Andersen story.

Emberley, Rebecca. *Three Cool Kids.*

> Three city goats encounter a disagreeable rat in this retelling of "The Billy Goats Gruff."

Ernst, Lisa Campbell. *Little Red Riding Hood: A Newfangled Prairie Tale.*

> This version takes place on the prairie where Grandma, a.k.a. *Big* Riding Hood, runs a farm.

Munsch, Robert. *The Paper Bag Princess.*

> A dragon takes the selfish prince and it's up to the princess to rescue him.

Scieszka, Jon. *The Frog Prince Continued.*

> The Frog Prince desperately tries to locate the proper witch who can turn him back into a frog.

Scieszka, Jon. *The True Story of the Three Little Pigs.*

> Here is the picture book that single-handedly revived the popularity of fractured fairy tales.

ADDITIONAL POEMS

"And After a Hundred Years Had Passed, Sleeping Beauty Awoke (at Last!) from Her Slumber" by Judith Viorst from *Sad Underwear and Other Complications*.

"And Then the Prince Knelt Down and Tried to Put the Glass Slipper on Cinderella's Foot" by Judith Viorst from *If I Were in Charge of the World*.

"Humpty Dumpty" by Jack Prelutsky from *For Laughing Out Loud*, edited by Jack Prelutsky.

"If Walt Whitman Had Written Humpty Dumpty" by William Cole from *Poem Stew*.

"In Search of Cinderella" by Shel Silverstein from *A Light in the Attic*.

"Mary Had a Little Lamb" from *Poems of A. Nonny Mouse*, edited by Jack Prelutsky.

"Mary Had a Stick of Gum" from *For Laughing Out Loud*, edited by Jack Prelutsky.

ADDITIONAL SONGS AND MUSICAL ACTIVITIES

"Flying 'Round the Mountain" by Joe Scruggs from *Even Trolls Have Moms*.

"Goldilocks Rap" by Bill Shontz from *Teddy Bear's Greatest Hits*.

"Jazzy Three Bears" by Cathy Fink from *Grandma Slid Down the Mountain*.

"The Three Little Pigs Blues" by Greg and Steve from *Playing Favorites*.

ADDITIONAL FINGERPLAYS AND MOVEMENT ACTIVITIES

"Two Little Black Birds"
traditional

1. Two little black birds sitting on a hill,
   (Hands behind back, thumbs up)

One named Jack and one named Jill.
(Bring out thumbs one at a time)
Fly away Jack,
(Hide one thumb)
Fly away Jill,
(Hide the other thumb)
Come back Jack,
(Bring back one thumb)
Come back Jill.
(Bring back the other thumb)

(Repeat with the following verses)

2. Two little black birds sitting on a pole,
   One named High and one named Low . . .
   (Hold one thumb overhead and one near the floor)

3. Two little black birds sitting on a pole,
   One named Fast and one named Slow . . .
   (Bring out one thumb quickly and the other slowly)

4. Two little black birds sitting on a gate,
   One named Early and one named Late . . .
   *(Bring out one thumb before you've finished saying
   the line and the other thumb several seconds after
   you've finished)*

VIDEOS

Goldilocks and the Three Bears. Weston Woods. (8 min.)

Red Riding Hood. Weston Woods. (8 min.)

The Three Little Pigs. Weston Woods. (12 min.)

Barnyard Fun

Program at a Glance

MUSIC	"Down on the Farm" from *We All Live Together, Vol. 5,* by Greg and Steve
MUSIC	"Old MacDonald" from *We've All Got Stories* by Jane Sapp
MUSICAL ACTIVITY	"When Cows Get Up in the Morning" from *Babes, Beasts and Birds* by Pat Carfra
PICTURE BOOK	*Barnyard Banter* by Denise Fleming
PICTURE BOOK	*Parents in the Pigpen, Pigs in the Tub* by Amy Ehrlich
POEM	"The Farm Is in a Flurry"
PICTURE BOOK	*Little Peep* by Jack Kent
MUSICAL ACTIVITY	"Oats and Beans and Barley Grow" from *Baby Beluga* by Raffi
PICTURE BOOK	*Farmer Duck* by Martin Waddell
MUSICAL ACTIVITY	"Down on Grandpa's Farm" from *Great Big Hits* by Sharon, Lois and Bram
MUSICAL ACTIVITY	"I Had a Rooster" from *Hello Everybody* by Rachel Buchman
PICTURE BOOK	*Barnyard Lullaby* by Frank Asch

Preparation and Presentation

In your publicity, ask audience members to bring their own stuffed farm animals. Decorate the story area with puppets or stuffed animals found on the farm. Don a John Deere cap, blue jeans, and work boots. As the audience enters the story area, play "Down on the Farm." Or play the funkiest version of "Old MacDonald" ever from the recording *We've All Got Stories* by Jane Sapp.

Ask the audience to "cock-a-doodle-doo" to begin the story program, much like the rooster does to start the new day on the farm.

"When Cows Get Up in the Morning"
traditional

This extremely simple call-and-response song will give the audience a chance to make more farm animal noises. Have the audience echo each line.

> When cows get up in the morning, they always say
>   "Good day,"
> Moo . . . moo . . . that's how they say "Good day."

Repeat with verses on pigs, donkeys, and any farm animals the audience suggests. End with something funny like a mosquito or elephant. Make up your own melody or chant or use the melody found on Pat Carfra's recording *Babes, Beasts, and Birds*.

Barnyard Banter
Denise Fleming

Don't stop making animal noises. With bright, bold illustrations, Fleming shows several more farm animals making their noises. The audience will automatically chime in.

Parents in the Pigpen, Pigs in the Tub
Amy Ehrlich

The farm animals decide they'd rather live inside the farm-house instead of the barn. The farm family puts up with this invasion until the pigs take over the bathroom.

"The Farm Is in a Flurry"
anonymous

> The farm is in a flurry,
> The rooster's caught the flu,
> His cock-a-doodle-do has changed
> To cock-a-doodle-CHOO!

Repeat the poem so the audience can share the sneeze noise.

Little Peep
Jack Kent

Little Peep believes he can "cock-a-doodle-doo" just as good as the conceited rooster. However, his attempt comes out as a high-pitched "PEEP-ADEEDLE-PEEP." The audience will be rolling on the floor, especially when the other animals give it a try with their "MOO-KA-DOODLE-MOOs" and "OINK-A-DIDDLE-OINKs."

"Oats and Beans and Barley Grow"
traditional

Recorded versions of this song can be found on Raffi's record-ing *Baby Beluga* and *Wee Sing and Play*.

Ask everyone to stand and make several small circles. Have them hold hands and walk in circles during the first verse.

> Oats and beans and barley grow, oats and beans and
>   barley grow,
> Do you or I or anyone know how oats and beans and
>   barley grow?"
> > *(Stop walking and perform the following motions)*

First the farmer sows the seed,
   (Pretend to plant a seed)

Then she stands and takes her ease,
   (Straighten up and "dust off" hands)

Stamps her foot and claps her hands
   (Stamp foot, clap hands)

And turns around to view the land.
   (Look with hand over eyes)

(Repeat the first verse with the circle walk)

Farmer Duck
Martin Waddell

A hardworking duck has the bad luck to work for a lazy farmer. The audience can "quack" when the farmer asks "How goes the work?" The other farm animals devise a plan to save the duck. This is one of my favorite picture books.

"Down on Grandpa's Farm"
traditional

The melody for this song can be found on the recording *A Cathy and Marcy Collection for Kids* by Cathy Fink and Marcy Marxer and on *Great Big Hits* by Sharon, Lois and Bram.

Down on Grandpa's farm there is a big, brown cow,
Down on Grandpa's farm there is a big, brown cow,
The cow, it goes a lot like this . . . "Moo!"
The cow, it goes a lot like this . . . "Moo!"
We're on our way, we're on our way, on our way to
   Grandpa's farm.
We're on our way, we're on our way, on our way to
   Grandpa's farm.

Ask the audience to suggest other farm animals for additional verses. Move on to nonfarm animal ideas, such as an alligator.

Down on Grandpa's farm, there is a green alligator . . .
The alligator, it goes a lot like this . . . SNAP!
   (Clap hands)

Ask the audience for nonanimal ideas. It can be anything that makes a noise, such as a robot or a spaceship or a lawn mower or a (back to the farm) tractor.

> Down on Grandpa's farm, there is an old tractor . . .
> The tractor, it goes a lot like this . . . "Putt-putt-wheeze-
>   pop-bang!"

 ## "I Had a Rooster"
traditional

Here's a chance to show off your puppet collection and the animals the audience brought. Ask for volunteers (get a variety of ages) to come to the front of the room. Give each volunteer a different animal. Place the farm animals first. If you don't have a rooster puppet, hold up a picture of a rooster and sing:

> I had a rooster, the rooster pleased me.
> I fed my rooster 'neath the old chestnut tree.
> My little rooster went "cock-a-doodle-doo, dee-doodle-
>   dee-doodle-dee-doodle-dee-doo."

Repeat verses for each of the puppets. Have the audience help with the animal noises.

> I had a donkey, the donkey pleased me.
> I fed my donkey 'neath the old chestnut tree.
> My little donkey went "Hee Haw,"
> My little rooster went "cock-a-doodle-doo, dee-doodle-dee-
>   doodle-dee-doodle-dee-doo."

The melody can be found on Rachel Buchman's recording *Hello Everybody* or Pat Carfra's *Babes, Beasts, and Birds.*

 ## *Barnyard Lullaby*
Frank Asch

Here's a good book to wind down the farm fun. Each farm animal in the book sings a lullaby to its baby. The farmer, however, only hears an animal racket and can't get to sleep until his wife sings a lullaby to their child. The lullaby score is included in the book.

Mix and Match

ADDITIONAL PICTURE BOOKS

Alarcon, Karen Beaumont. *Louella Mae, She's Run Away*.

> The whole farmhouse searches high and low for Louella Mae. The rhymed text is designed to let the audience guess the various locations the characters search.

Barnes-Murphy, Rowan. *Old MacDonald Had a Farm.*

> Lift-the-flaps reveal dancing pigs, trumpet-playing sheep, donkeys with maracas, and cows in the bathtub in this silly picture book version of the popular song.

Ernst, Lisa Campbell. *When Bluebell Sang.*

> Bluebell the cow has a sweet and clear singing voice. She soon finds herself onstage singing before huge crowds and trapped by an unethical agent.

Johnston, Tony. *Farmer Mack Measures His Pig.*

> Farmer Mack declares that his pig is the fattest pig alive, and he sets out to prove it. The audience will have an opportunity to make pig-calling noises.

King, P. E. *Down on the Funny Farm.*

> The cat whinnies, the horse crows "cock-a-doodle-doo," the rooster barks, the dog sits on a nest of eggs, the chicken oinks, and the pig chases mice.

Lillie, Patricia. *When the Rooster Crowed.*

> A farmer puts off getting out of bed until the very last minute.

ADDITIONAL POEMS

"Baby Chick" by Aileen Fisher from *Eric Carle's Animals Animals,* edited by Eric Carle.

"Dimpleton the Simpleton" by Dennis Lee from *The Ice Cream Store.*

"The Farmer and the Queen" by Shel Silverstein from *Where the Sidewalk Ends.*

"The Prayer of the Little Duck" by Carmen Bernos de Gasztold from *Animal Crackers: A Delightful Collection of Pictures, Poems, and Lullabies for the Very Young,* edited by Jane Dyer.

"Quack! Said the Billy Goat" by Charles Causley from *Eric Carle's Animals Animals,* edited by Eric Carle.

ADDITIONAL SONGS AND MUSICAL ACTIVITIES

"Barnyard Dance" by John McCutcheon from *Mail Myself to You.*

"Cluck, Cluck, Red Hen" by Raffi from *Corner Grocery Store.*

Did You Feed My Cow?" by Sharon, Lois and Bram from *Smorgasbord.*

"Heading on Down to the Barn" by Red Grammer from *Down the Do-Re-Mi.*

"On the Funny Farm" by Rosenshontz from *Uh-Oh.*

ADDITIONAL FINGERPLAYS AND MOVEMENT ACTIVITIES

"The Little Ducklings"
Elizabeth Vollrath

(Line up and walk around like ducks as the poem indicates)

All the little ducklings
Line up in a row.
Quack, quack, quack,
And away they go.

They follow their mother
Waddling to and fro.
Quack, quack, quack,
And away they go.

Down to the big pond
Happy as can be.
Quack, quack, quack,
They are full of glee.

They jump in the water
And bob up and down.
Quack, quack, quack,
They swim all around.

All the little ducklings
Swimming far away.
Quack, quack, quack,
They'll play another day.

"This Little Cow"
traditional

(Have the big folks wiggle the toes of the little folks much like "This Little Piggy." Start with the little toe.)

This little cow eats grass,
This little cow eats hay,
This little cow looks over the hedge,
This little cow runs away,
And this **Big Cow** does nothing
But lie in the field all day.

VIDEOS

The Day Jimmy's Boa Ate the Wash. Weston Woods. (5 min.)

Rosie's Walk. Weston Woods. (4 min.)

Big & Gray

Program at a Glance

MUSIC	"If You Love a Hippopotamus" from *Bellybutton* by Heather Bishop
POEM	"A Baby Rhinoceros" from *The Other Side of the Door* by Jeff Moss
PICTURE BOOK	*A Porcupine Named Fluffy* by Helen Lester
FELT STORY	"The Fearsome Beast" adapted by Judy Sierra from *The Flannel Board Storytelling Book*
PICTURE BOOK	*The Biggest Nose* by Kathy Caple
MOVEMENT ACTIVITY	"An Elephant Goes Like This and That"
PICTURE BOOK	*Seven Blind Mice* by Ed Young
PICTURE BOOK	*What Could a Hippopotamus Be?* by Mike Thaler
POEM	"Recipe for a Hippopotamus Sandwich" from *Where the Sidewalk Ends* by Shel Silverstein
MOVEMENT ACTIVITY	"Elephant Hunt"
MUSIC	"Baby Elephant Walk" from *All Time Greatest Hits* by Henry Mancini

Preparation and Presentation

Play "If You Love a Hippopotamus" as the audience enters the story area. Once everyone has settled down, tell a classic elephant riddle.

What happened when an elephant took the bus?
(The police made him give it back.)

Here are a few more elephant riddles. You can easily change them into hippo or rhino riddles. Sprinkle them throughout the program to elicit good-natured groans.

What do elephants have that no other animals have?
(Baby elephants)

Why did the elephant lie in the middle of the road?
(To trip the ants)

Why did the elephant lie in the middle of the road with his feet in the air?
(To trip the birds)

What time is it when an elephant sits in your car?
(Time to buy a new car)

How can you tell when an elephant's in the bathtub with you?
(By the smell of peanuts on its breath)

If you don't like any of the above elephant riddles, there are hundreds more lurking in your library's jokes and riddles collections.

"A Baby Rhinoceros"
Jeff Moss

This poem is perfect for this story theme because it contains humorous references to all three "big and gray" creatures.

A Porcupine Named Fluffy
Helen Lester

A little porcupine named Fluffy worries about his name. Then he meets a rhinoceros named Hippo. Your audience will enjoy the porcupine's parents' attempts to name him, with suggestions ranging from "Spike" and "Prickles" to "Needleroozer."

"The Fearsome Beast"
adapted by Judy Sierra

The story is similar to Verna Aardema's picture book *Who's in Rabbit's House?* Caterpillar pretends that he is a fierce warrior who can "crush the rhinoceros to earth" and "make dust of the elephant." Patterns for the felt pieces, including those for rhino and elephant, can be found in Sierra's book.

The Biggest Nose
Kathy Caple

Eleanor the elephant's classmates make fun of her big nose. She tries to hide it until she learns that she has a nice nose after all. There are several opportunities to use a wonderful elephant trumpeting noise in this book of self-esteem. Check out Frederick Newman's book *Mouthsounds*. He gives step-by-step instructions on how to make the "cool" elephant trumpet noise.

"An Elephant Goes Like This and That"
traditional

> An elephant goes like this
> > *(Stomp left foot)*
> and that.
> > *(Stomp right foot)*
> He's terribly huge,
> > *(Hold arms overhead)*
> He's terribly fat.
> > *(Hold arms in front)*
> He has no fingers,
> > *(Wiggle fingers)*

He has no toes,
> *(Wiggle toes)*

But goodness gracious,
What a nose!
> *(Hold arm in front of nose like a trunk. Here's a good time to unleash that elephant noise you've mastered.)*

Seven Blind Mice
Ed Young

The audience will guess that the "strange something" in the story is actually an elephant long before the book's mice characters do.

What Could a Hippopotamus Be?
Mike Thaler

Your audience will soon discover that a hippopotamus *cannot* be a fireman climbing a ladder, a sailor in a tiny rowboat, or several other "lightweight" occupations.

"Recipe for a Hippopotamus Sandwich"
Shel Silverstein

Draw or paste a picture of a hippo on a piece of poster board. Draw or paste pictures of two slices of bread on the top and bottom of the hippo. Tape the text of Silverstein's short poem on the back of the poster board and read it with the hippo picture out of sight of the audience. On the last line, hold up the picture for the audience to see.

Another possibility is to tie two actual pieces of bread on a hippo puppet while you recite the poem. Either way makes for a fun way to slip yet another poem into the program.

"Elephant Hunt"
Rob Reid

Instead of leading your audience on a traditional bear hunt, why not take them on an elephant hunt? The audience travels through mud and water before coming face to face with an elephant. (And, of course, there are plenty of opportunities to make the elephant trumpeting noise that everyone has mastered through the course of the program.)

Have hunters slap their legs to simulate walking.

Chorus:
> We're going on an elephant hunt, we're going on an
>   elephant hunt,
> We'll stomp and sway and *(elephant trumpeting noise)*
>   all day,
> We're going on an elephant hunt.

Where are we going to find an elephant? At the zoo!
> Let's go!

(Chorus)

Stop! Look over there . . . in the children's zoo . . . in
>   that big mud puddle . . .
Something big and gray. Maybe it's an elephant. Let's go
>   over.
Hope you don't mind walking in the mud.
> *(Make squishing noises)*
Get your cameras out.
Ready! Aim! WAIT! Listen!
> *(Make pig noise)*
That's not an elephant, it's a . . .
> *(Audience shouts)* Pig!
Everyone, out of the mud!
> *(Make squishing noises)*
Oh no, look at our feet. What a mess. Just scrape the mud
>   off with your hands.
> *(Mime scraping the mud off)*
Oh no, look at our hands. What a mess. Just wipe it off
>   on your shirt.
> *(Mime wiping mud off hands)*
On your neighbor's shirt.
> *(Wipe hands on neighbor)*
Let's go to another part of the zoo.

(Chorus)

Stop! Look over there . . . by that big tank of water . . .
Something big and gray. Maybe it's an elephant.
Let's tiptoe and get a closer look.
>*(Whisper)* Tiptoe, tiptoe.

Get your cameras out.
Ready! Aim! WAIT!
>*(Make the barking sound of a seal—Ark! Ark! Ark!)*

That's not an elephant! That's a . . .
>*(Audience shouts)* Seal!

Let's go to another part of the zoo.
Look at the time! We'll never make it at this rate.
We have to go faster.

(Recite the chorus fast)

Faster!

(Recite the chorus faster)

FASTER!

(Recite the chorus as a mumbled blur. Start gasping for breath.)

I need to rest against this big gray wall.
>*(Stand with arms outstretched leaning against "the gray wall")*

I usually have someone in the audience catch on right away and yell out "The wall is an elephant!" If they don't, I'll say something like "This wall feels funny." It doesn't take much for them to realize that I'm leaning against an elephant.

An elephant? Let's get outta here!

>*(Everyone screams)*

(Aside): Didn't you always want to scream in a
>library?

Whew, we're safe. Wait a minute! We forgot something.
>*(Audience yells out)* We forgot to take a picture!

You know what that means, don't you? It means . . .

(Chorus)

We're going on an elephant hunt, we're going on an
   elephant hunt,
We'll stomp and sway and *(feeble elephant trumpet noise)*
   all day,
We're going on an elephant hunt.
TOMORROW!

Tell one last elephant riddle.

 ### "Baby Elephant Walk"
Henry Mancini

Play Henry Mancini's "Baby Elephant Walk" found on his recording *All Time Greatest Hits*. Lead everyone out of the story area, single file, with exaggerated hip movement and arms simulating trunks, for a closing elephant parade.

Mix and Match

ADDITIONAL PICTURE BOOKS

Hadithi, Mwenye. *Hot Hippo*.

   Hippo asks the permission of Ngai the God of Everything
   and Everywhere to live in the water.

Martin, Bill, Jr. *The Happy Hippopotami*.

   The hippopotamamas and the hippopotapoppas join all of
   the other hippopotami on the beach.

Rosen, Michael. *How Giraffe Got Such a Long Neck and Why
Rhino Is So Grumpy*.

   Giraffe and Rhino ask Man to help them reach the leaves
   at the top of the trees. Rhino becomes very cross when he
   doesn't receive a long neck like Giraffe.

Silverstein, Shel. *Who Wants a Cheap Rhinoceros?*

> There are a lot of wonderful reasons for having a rhino around the house. Scratching backs with his horn, acting as a coat hanger, and jump rope twirling are just a few of his many talents.

Thomas, Patricia. *"Stand Back," Said the Elephant, "I'm Going to Sneeze."*

> The animals are worried when Elephant announces that he has to sneeze. Disaster strikes when he instead starts his earth-shaking laughter.

ADDITIONAL POEMS

"An Elephant Is Hard to Hide" by Jack Prelutsky from *Something Big Has Been Here.*

"The Handiest Nose" by Aileen Fisher from *Side by Side: Poems to Read Together,* edited by Lee Bennett Hopkins.

"Hippopotamus" by Mary Ann Hoberman from *Yellow Butter, Purple Jelly, Red Jam, Black Bread.*

"Holding Hands" by Lenore M. Link from *Read Aloud Rhymes for the Very Young,* edited by Jack Prelutsky.

"I Want a Pet Porcupine, Mother" by Jack Prelutsky from *Something Big Has Been Here.*

"The Rhinoceros" by Ogden Nash from *Once upon a Rhyme,* edited by Sara and Stephen Corrin.

"What Fun to Be a Hippopotamus" by Michael Flanders from *Eric Carle's Animals Animals,* edited by Eric Carle.

ADDITIONAL SONGS AND MUSICAL ACTIVITIES

"Don't Be Rude to a Rhinoceros" by Tom Paxton from *I've Got a Yo-Yo.*

"Englebert the Elephant" by Tom Paxton from *Goin' to the Zoo.*

"Hippo Hooray" by Linda Arnold from *Happiness Cake*.

"Hippopotamus Rock" by Rosenshontz from *Rosenshontz Tickles You*.

"Otto the Hippo" by Fred Penner from *Collections*.

ADDITIONAL FINGERPLAYS AND MOVEMENT ACTIVITIES

"One Elephant Went Out to Play"
traditional, adapted by Rob Reid

(The tune can be found on *Great Big Hits* by Sharon, Lois and Bram.)

> One elephant went out to play,
> > *(Hold up one finger)*
> Upon a spider's web one day.
> > *(Spread fingers on both hands. Touch fingertips to simulate a web)*
> He had such enormous fun,
> > *(Hold arm in front of nose for a "trunk")*
> That he called for more to come.
> > *(Wave "trunk" for "more to come")*
>
> An elephant and a hippo
> Went out to play,
> > *(Hold up two fingers)*
> Upon a spider's web one day.
> > *(Make "web" with fingers)*
> They had such enormous fun
> > *(Hold both arms out, elbows stacked on each other in front of chest for a "hippo mouth")*
> That they called for more to come.
> > *(Wave for "more to come")*
>
> An elephant, a hippo, and a rhino
> Went out to play,
> > *(Hold up three fingers)*

Upon a spider's web one day.
    (Make "web" with fingers)
They had such enormous fun
    (Hold hand outward on nose for a "rhino horn")
But they all said, "We are done."
    (Wave goodbye)

"Way Down South"
traditional, adapted by Rob Reid

Way down South
    (Point down)
Where bananas grow,
    (Spread fingers downward)
A flea stepped on
    (Wave pinkie finger)
An elephant's toe.
    (Wave foot)
The elephant cried
With tears in his eyes,
    (Wipe away tears)
"Why don't you pick on
Someone your size?"
    (Talk to pinkie finger in front of you)

VIDEOS

The Circus Baby. Weston Woods. (5 min.)

Hot Hippo. Weston Woods. (6 min.)

Birdland

— **Program at a Glance** —

MUSIC	"This Song Is for the Birds" from *The Happy Wanderer* by Bill Staines
POEM	"The Little Birds"
PICTURE BOOK	*Birdsong* by Audrey Wood
MUSIC	"Billy Magee Magaw"
PICTURE BOOK	*Six Crows* by Leo Lionni
MUSICAL ACTIVITY	"Three Craw" from *The Elephant Show Record* by Sharon, Lois and Bram
PICTURE BOOK	*Duckat* by Gaelyn Gordon
MUSICAL ACTIVITY	"Five Little Ducks" from *Hello Everybody* by Rachel Buchman
PICTURE BOOK	*Tacky the Penguin* by Helen Lester
PICTURE BOOK	*The Paper Crane* by Molly Bang
CRAFT	Origami bird patterns in *Paper Pandas and Jumping Frogs* by Florence Temko

Preparation and Presentation

As the audience enters the story area, play the recording "This Song Is for the Birds." Another option is to play a nature-sounds recording that features bird calls. These are available in nature shops. Ask the audience to make their best bird noises. Listen to the variety from whistles and chirps to clucks and squawks. Perhaps you'll even get a loon call. Play a duck call if you have one.

Next, ask the kids if they know what baby birds look like when they are hungry. Have them imitate the outstretched mouths of baby birds at feeding time. Have the children close their mouths. When their parents pretend to hold up worms, the kids should open their mouths in great anticipation. This will get them ready for the opening poem.

"The Little Birds"
traditional

> The little birds sit in their nests and beg,
> All mouth that once had been all egg.

Birdsong
Audrey Wood

The audience can refine their bird noises. Different birds make their unique calls in this gentle book with lovely, two-page picture spreads for each bird.

"Billy Magee Magaw"
traditional

The audience can now narrow their bird call talents to raucous "caw's." Sing this ditty to the tune of "When Johnny Comes Marching Home" (as found on *The Civil War: Original Soundtrack Recording*).

> There were three crows sat on a tree,
> Billy Magee Magaw.
> There were three crows sat on a tree,
> Billy Magee Magaw.

There were three crows sat on a tree,
They were as black as crows could be,
And they all flapped their wings and cried
"Caw, caw, caw!"

Six Crows
Leo Lionni

A farmer and several crows battle over a wheat crop. The battle soon escalates with scarier and scarier scarecrows and bigger and bigger "scare-birds." Draw a picture of a simple scarecrow as you read the story. Draw a second figure in the shape of a simple bird. A marker board would work best with this story. As the battle between the farmer and the crows grows, make the two figures bigger and meaner. Draw a fierce frown on the scarecrow. When the owl finally leads the warring sides to peace, erase the scarecrow's frown and replace it with a smile.

"Three Craw"
traditional

Tell the audience that a Scottish term for crow is "craw." Make three simple felt crows out of triangles and circles. Use one triangle for the body, a smaller triangle for the tail, a circle for the head, and a tiny triangle for the beak. Remove the felt "craws" one by one during the course of the song.

1. Three craw sat upon a wall,
    Sat upon a wall, sat upon a wall,
    Three craw sat upon a wall

    Chorus:
        On a cold and frosty morning.

(Continue with the following verses)

2. The first craw couldn't find his ma . . .
3. The second craw fell and broke his jaw . . .

4. The third craw 'et the other twa . . .

5. The fourth craw was not there at all . . .

6. And that's all I heard about the craw . . .

Duckat

Gaelyn Gordon

A girl named Mabel finds a wild duck that thinks it's a cat. It meows, drinks milk, and chases mice. Mabel checks her "Doctor Book" under the heading "What to do for a duck that thinks it is a cat."

"Five Little Ducks"

traditional

Recorded versions of the song can be found on Rachel Buchman's recording *Hello Everybody* and on two Raffi recordings—*Rise and Shine* and *Raffi in Concert with the Rise and Shine Band*.

Have everyone stand up and waddle around like ducks, or have the audience form one or two lines and waddle. Lead one of the lines yourself. Consider changing the opening line from "Five little ducks" to "Lots of little ducks."

Five little ducks that I once knew,
Fat ones, skinny ones, tall ones too.
But the one little duck with the feather on her back
    (Wave hands behind backs)
She led the others with a
"Quack, quack, quack—
    (Have audience "quack" by opening and shutting
    their hands on each "quack")
Quack, quack, quack—
Quack, quack, quack,"
She led the others with a
"Quack, quack, quack."

Down to the river they would go,
Wibble-wobble, wibble-wobble, to and fro,
  (Exaggerate waddling)
But the one little duck
With the feather on her back
  (Wave hands behind backs)
She led the others with a
"Quack, quack, quack—
  (Make hand motions for quacks)
Quack, quack, quack—
Quack, quack, quack,"
She led the others with a
"Quack, quack, quack."

Up from the river they would come,
Wibble-wobble, wibble-wobble, to and fro,
  (Exaggerate waddling)
But the one little duck
With the feather on her back
  (Wave hands behind backs)
She led the others with a
"Quack, quack, quack—
  (Make hand motions for quacks)
Quack, quack, quack—
Quack, quack, quack,"
She led the others with a
"Quack, quack, quack."

Tacky the Penguin
Helen Lester

After waddling like a duck, try waddling like a penguin (hands close at sides—almost Chaplinesque). This is a fun story to act out as you tell it.

Tacky is a little different from the other penguins: Goodly, Lovely, Angel, Neatly, and Perfect. While the others dive grace-fully into the water, Tacky does a cannonball. When the others march in a straight line 1-2-3, Tacky wobbles 1-2-3-4-2-3-6.

The Paper Crane
Molly Bang

An old man pays for his meal with an origami crane. The crane magically comes to life. Read the story or play the *Reading Rainbow* video, which shows the story in a five-minute segment.

 ### Origami Birds

Follow *The Paper Crane* with a simple origami demonstration. The crane figure is hard to teach, but many origami books and videos show how to create simple bird figures. Find one that you or a volunteer can make, and teach it to the audience. Bring typing paper or gift-wrap paper or purchase origami paper from an art supply store. The adults can help the children follow your directions.

If you wish to make a crane figure, a pattern can be found in Florence Temko's book *Paper Pandas and Jumping Frogs.* The thirty-minute video *How to Fold a Paper Crane* is another good instructional resource.

Mix and Match

ADDITIONAL PICTURE BOOKS

Eastman, P. D. *Are You My Mother?*

A baby bird asks various animals—and a steam shovel—if they are his mother.

Ehlert, Lois. *Feathers for Lunch.*

A cat stalks several North American backyard birds. The birds are warned by the cat's jingling bell. All the cat manages to catch are "feathers for lunch."

Kent, Jack. *Round Robin.*

Robin eats so much he becomes too heavy to fly. Instead, he moves "hippety, hoppety, boppety, BUMP." As winter nears, Robin has no choice but to "hop" south for the winter.

Lester, Helen. *Three Cheers for Tacky.*

> Tacky the penguin is back. His friends enter a Penguin Cheering Contest. Naturally, Tacky messes up the precision cheer. The audience will soon learn the cheer and chime "1-2-3 LEFT! 1-2-3 RIGHT! Stand up! Sit down! Say 'Good Night!'"

Ward, Helen. *The King of the Birds.*

> The birds decide to choose a king but can't decide how to pick one. They finally decide that the king will be the bird who can fly the highest. Eagle soars above the rest, but when he tires, Wren flies out from his hiding spot on Eagle's back to fly even higher. The bold, colorful illustrations show an incredible array of birds.

ADDITIONAL POEMS

"Barn Owl" by Marilyn Singer from *Turtle in July.*

"Birdseed" by Brod Bagert from *For Laughing Out Loud,* edited by Jack Prelutsky.

"The Duck" by Ogden Nash from *Custard and Company.*

"Early Bird" by Shel Silverstein from *Where the Sidewalk Ends.*

"Humming Birds" by Betty Sage from *Read-Aloud Rhymes for the Very Young,* edited by Jack Prelutsky.

"Hungry Morning" by Myra Cohn Livingston from *The Sky Is Full of Song,* edited by Lee Bennett Hopkins.

"Kiwi" by Doug Florian from *Beast Feast.*

"Sparrow" by Kaye Starbird from *Eric Carle's Animals Animals,* edited by Eric Carle.

ADDITIONAL SONGS AND MUSICAL ACTIVITIES

"Bahamas Pajamas" by Joe Scruggs from *Bahamas Pajamas.*

"Butts Up" by Banana Slug String Band from *Slugs at Sea.*

"The Crow That Wanted to Sing" by Tom Paxton from *I've Got a Yo-Yo.*

"Migratin' " by Sally Rogers from *What Can One Little Person Do?*

"Songbirds" by Jack Grunsky from *Jumpin' Jack.*

ADDITIONAL FINGERPLAYS AND MOVEMENT ACTIVITIES

"Five Little Birdies"
traditional

> Five little birdies lived in a tree,
> Father,
>> *(Hold up one finger)*
> Mother,
>> *(Hold up second finger)*
> And babies three.
>> *(Hold up three more fingers)*
> Father caught a worm,
>> *(Wiggle one finger)*
> Mother caught a bug,
>> *(Wiggle hand)*
> The three little babies
> Began to tug.
>> *(Mime tugging)*
> One got the bug,
>> *(Wiggle hand)*
> One got the worm,
>> *(Wiggle finger)*
> The last one said
> "Hey! When's my turn?"
>> *(Cross arms)*

"A Wise Old Owl"
traditional

> A wise old owl sat in an oak,
> > *(Circle hands around eyes)*
> The more he heard,
> > *(Cup ears)*
> The less he spoke.
> > *(Cover mouth)*
> The less he spoke,
> The more he heard.
> > *(Cup ears)*
> Why aren't we all like that
> Wise old bird?
> > *(Shrug shoulders)*

VIDEOS

How to Fold a Paper Crane. Informed Democracy. Asia for Kids distributor. (800) 888-9681. (30 min.)

The Paper Crane. Reading Rainbow. (5 min.)

Peeping Beauty. Living Oak Media. (9 min.)

The Story about Ping. Weston Woods. (10 min.)

Black Bears, Brown Bears, Polar, Panda, & Teddy Bears

Program at a Glance

MUSIC	"Teddy Bear's Picnic" from *Not for Kids Only* by Jerry Garcia and David Grissman
POEM	"Fuzzy Wuzzy"
PICTURE BOOK	*Goldilocks and the Three Bears* by James Marshall
POEM	"Porridge" from *The Three Bears Rhyme Book* by Jane Yolen
PICTURE BOOK	*My Brown Bear Barney* by Dorothy Butler
MOVEMENT ACTIVITY	"Bear Hunt" by Rob Reid
PICTURE BOOK	*Poppy the Panda* by Dick Gackenbach
POEM	"Bear in There" from *A Light in the Attic* by Shel Silverstein
PICTURE BOOK	*Little Mo* by Martin Waddell
MOVEMENT ACTIVITY	"Teddy Bear Rap"

Preparation and Presentation

Invite the public to attend a celebration of bears by bringing their own teddy bears.

The adults will love to hear Jerry Garcia singing "Teddy Bear's Picnic." Other possibilities are the recordings *Unbearable Bears* by Kevin Roth and *Teddy Bear's Greatest Hits* by Bill Shontz, both full of bear songs.

"Fuzzy Wuzzy"

Many family members know this four-line ditty. It should set the tone for the silliness to follow.

> Fuzzy Wuzzy was a bear.
> Fuzzy Wuzzy had no hair.
> Fuzzy Wuzzy wasn't fuzzy,
> Was he?

Goldilocks and the Three Bears
James Marshall

This is one of the funniest contemporary versions of the story. When Goldilocks notices brown fur all around, she assumes the home owners have "kitties."

"Porridge"
Jane Yolen

Ask the children if they know what porridge is. I've had answers range from "soup" to "rocks." Yolen's poem is a nostalgic look at the word that is especially geared for parents.

> There are always three bowls,
> And always three spoons,
> And Momma Bear humming
> Her wake-me-up tunes.
> There are always three napkins,
> Always three chairs,
> And the great big yawns
> Of breakfasting bears.

As far or as old
As I grow to be,
That's what porridge
Will mean to me.

My Brown Bear Barney
Dorothy Butler

A little girl takes a lot of possessions to various places, but she always remembers to take her "brown bear Barney." The audience will soon chant this refrain right before they all go "Aw-w-w."

"Bear Hunt"
adapted by Rob Reid

Bear hunts (or lion hunts or dragon hunts) have been long-time popular storytime activities. Here's a version in which the audience pretends that they are bear cubs going on an adventure. Have the audience slap their legs and echo the lines.

Chorus:

> We're bear cubs going on a bear hunt.
> Gonna have a lot of fun.
> What a big adventure.
> C'mon everyone.

Bye warm cave.
> *(Wave goodbye)*
Through tall grass.
Swish-swish, swish-swish.
> *(Move hands as if going through tall grass)*

(Chorus)

Into the stream. Very wet.
Splash-splash, splash-splash.
> *(Make splashing motions with hands)*

(Chorus)

Hollow log. Grubs inside.
Crawl-crawl, crawl-crawl.
> *(Pretend to crawl)*

(Chorus)

Here's a bog. Watch your step.
Squish-squash, squish-squash.
> *(Move hands as if they were feet getting stuck)*

(Chorus)

Up a tree. What can we see?
Climb-climb, climb-climb.
> *(Make climbing motions)*

What's that smell?
> *(Sniff the air)*

Sure smells good.
Down-down, down-down.
> *(Climb down)*

There's the food. Let's go eat.
> *(Point)*

Yum-yum, yum-yum.
> *(Pretend to eat)*

What's that noise?
> *(Cup ears)*

Look!
> *(Point)*

Strange creatures. They have two legs. They have two
arms.
Run!
> *(Slap legs quickly. Act out the following motions
> hurriedly)*

Back up the tree. Climb-climb.
> *(Climbing motions)*

Back down the tree. Down-down.
> *(Climb down)*

Through the bog. Squish-squash.

Through the log. Crawl-crawl.
   (Crawl)
Through the stream. Splash-splash.
Through the grass. Swish-swish.
Safe at last. Our nice warm cave.
We're bear cubs and we were on a bear hunt.
What a big adventure.

Poppy the Panda
Dick Gackenbach

Use props with this story. Poppy the stuffed panda asks Katie if he can wear something special. Katie tries to dress Poppy in roller skates, dresses, and pots—even toilet paper—to no avail. As you read or tell the story, drape these props on a stuffed toy panda.

"Bear in There"
Shel Silverstein

There's a polar bear in a refrigerator. Tape two pieces of white poster board together to make a crude "refrigerator." Paste a picture of a polar bear on the inside of the refrigerator and paste a copy of the poem on the back. When you read the section of the poem about opening the door, lift the top poster board, show the bear picture, roar, and slam the "door" shut. Finish the poem with an exasperated voice.

Little Mo
Martin Waddell

This follow-up to the polar bear poem is about a polar bear cub who tries ice skating with disastrous results.

"Teddy Bear Rap"
End the program with a rap version of the traditional activity "Teddy Bear, Teddy Bear, Turn around." Put sunglasses on one of your teddy bears and have it lead the audience in the following activity (done in a rap cadence, of course):

Teddy Bear, Teddy Bear, turn around.
Teddy Bear, Teddy Bear, touch the ground.
Teddy Bear, Teddy Bear, show your shoe.
Teddy Bear, Teddy Bear, that will do.
Teddy Bear, Teddy Bear, climb the stairs.
Teddy Bear, Teddy Bear, say your prayers.
Teddy Bear, Teddy Bear, turn out the light.
Teddy Bear, Teddy Bear, say "Goodnight."

Mix and Match

ADDITIONAL PICTURE BOOKS

Alborough, Jez. *Where's My Teddy?*

A boy loses his teddy bear in the woods and encounters a giant teddy bear that was lost by a gigantic bear.

Arnosky, Jim. *Every Autumn Comes the Bear.*

A black bear appears in the woods behind a farm every autumn after the leaves have fallen.

Asch, Frank. *Sand Cake.*

Baby Bear and Papa Bear use their imaginations to create a cake on the beach.

Hayes, Sarah. *This Is the Bear.*

A teddy bear is accidentally taken to the garbage dump.

Kraus, Robert. *Milton, the Early Riser*.

A panda cub wakes up before all of the other animals.

Rosen, Michael. *We're Going on a Bear Hunt.*

A family goes out on the traditional bear hunt.

ADDITIONAL POEMS

"Bears" by Elizabeth Coatsworth from *An Arkful of Animals,* edited by William Cole.

"Furry Bear" by A. A. Milne from *An Arkful of Animals*, edited by William Cole.

"Grizzly Bear" by Mary Austin from *Bear in Mind: A Book of Bear Poems*, edited by Bobbye Goldstein.

"Honey Bear" by Elizabeth Lang from *Poems for the Very Young*, edited by Michael Rosen.

"If a Grizzly Bear Had Feathers" by Jeff Moss from *The Other Side of the Door*.

"My Teddy Bear" by Margaret Hillert from *Read-Aloud Rhymes for the Very Young*, edited by Jack Prelutsky.

"Night Bear" by Lee Bennett Hopkins from *Surprises*.

ADDITIONAL SONGS AND MUSICAL ACTIVITIES

"The Bear That Snores" by Kevin Roth from *Unbearable Bears*.

"The Bear Went over the Mountain" by Kevin Roth from *Oscar, Bingo and Buddies*.

"Grizzly Bear" from *Wee Sing Fun 'n' Folk*.

"One Shoe Bear" by Rosenshontz from *It's the Truth*.

"Waltzing with Bears" by Priscilla Herdman from *Stardreamer*.

VIDEOS

Beady Bear. Living Oak Media. (8 min.)

Corduroy. Weston Woods. (17 min.)

Bubbly Bubble Bathtime

Program at a Glance

MUSICAL ACTIVITY	"Rubber Duckie" from *Splish Splash: Bath Time Fun* by Sesame Street
MUSIC	"I'm a Dirty Kid" from *Hello Rachel! Hello Children!* by Rachel Buchman
PICTURE BOOK	*Mrs. Piggle-Wiggle's Won't-Take-a-Bath-Cure* by Betty MacDonald
POEM	"After a Bath" from *Always Wondering: Favorite Poems of Aileen Fisher* by Aileen Fisher
PICTURE BOOK	*King Bidgood's in the Bathtub* by Audrey Wood
PICTURE BOOK	*Five Minute's Peace* by Jill Murphy
POEM	"Naughty Soap Song" by Dorothy Aldis from *Read-Aloud Rhymes for the Very Young* edited by Jack Prelutsky
PICTURE BOOK	*Dad's Car Wash* by Harry A. Sutherland
MUSICAL ACTIVITY	"Head, Shoulders, Knees, and Toes" adapted by Joanie Bartels from *Bathtime Magic*
PICTURE BOOK	*Is It Time?* by Marilyn Janovitz
MUSIC	"Here We Go Loop 'D Loo" from *We All Live Together, Vol. 1,* by Greg and Steve

Preparation and Presentation

Play the song "Rubber Duckie" as the audience enters the story area. It can be found on several Sesame Street recordings including *Splish Splash: Bath Time Fun* and *Jim Hensen: A Sesame Street Celebration*. Show up in a robe with slippers and a shower cap. Carry a long-handled scrub brush, wash rag, towel, and of course, a rubber ducky. If you have access to a plastic infant bathtub, set it out and fill it with the picture books you'll be reading.

"I'm a Dirty Kid"
Rachel Buchman

Greet your audience, tell them to repeat everything they hear, and without saying another word, play the recording of "I'm a Dirty Kid." This call-and-response song is deceptively simple. Many parents report back to us that the kids won't stop singing it.

Have the audience echo each line. This can also be done as a chant.

Mrs. Piggle Wiggle's Won't-Take-a-Bath-Cure
Betty MacDonald

Patsy Brown refuses to take a bath. Wise Mrs. Piggle Wiggle convinces Patsy's parents to let Patsy stop taking baths. Patsy eventually gets so dirty that radishes grow on her skin. This story can also be found in the MacDonald chapter book *Mrs. Piggle Wiggle*.

"After a Bath"
Aileen Fisher

Have the audience stand and act out the poem's motions, such as drying fingers and toes and shaking like a dog.

King Bidgood's in the Bathtub
Audrey Wood

A king refuses to get out of the bathtub. Ask the parents if they ever had that problem with their kids. This excellent story with gorgeous, detailed illustrations is also performed as a mini-opera in filmstrip, video, and sound cassette formats.

Five Minute's Peace
Jill Murphy

Mother Elephant pleads with her three young children for just five minutes of peace and solitude. She relaxes in the tub but is soon joined by all three kids before her five minutes are up.

"Naughty Soap Song"
Dorothy Aldis

A bar of soap gets thinner and thinner in the bathtub. Tape a copy of the poem (unless you plan to memorize it) on the bottom of an infant-size tub. Place a full bar of soap and hide a second tiny sliver of a bar of soap in the tub. As you read the poem, toss the large bar of soap in the air as if it was very slippery. Drop it in the tub and pull out the sliver of soap for the last line: "my soap's growing thinner each day."

Dad's Car Wash
Harry Sutherland

A boy and his dad pretend that the bathtub is a car wash and the boy is a car. Instruct the parents to act out the bathing motions on their kids as you read about washing the hub caps (knees), the turn signals (ears), and the hood ornament (nose).

"Head, Shoulders, Knees, and Toes"
traditional, adapted by Joanie Bartels

Bartels has children wash their heads, shoulders, knees, and toes.

Have everyone stand for a bathtime version of "Heads, Shoulders, Knees, and Toes." Instead of simply pointing to these body parts, pretend to scrub them with an imaginary washcloth.

Wash your head and shoulders, knees and toes, knees and
  toes,
Head and shoulders, knees and toes, knees and toes, and
Eyes and ears and mouth and nose,
Head and shoulders, knees and toes, knees and toes.

Nancy Cassidy, on her recording *Kids Songs 2*, adds lines for
"Ankles, elbows, feet and seat" with "Hair and hips and chins
and cheeks" comprising the middle section. Parents and children alike will be hard pressed to keep up, but they'll all be
giggling. Challenge the older kids to lead the way.

Is It Time?
Marilyn Janovitz

Read the book as a call-and-response chant. The story
includes verses about toweling off, brushing "fangs" (the
young protagonist is a wolf), getting into bed, howling, and
getting a good night kiss—all of which can be acted out by the
audience. Add your own line after the book is done: "Is it time
to check out books? Yes, it's time to check out books! But first,
we have one last song to sing."

"Here We Go Loop 'D Loo"
traditional

Not many folks know that this popular song is actually about
taking a Saturday night bath. "You put your right hand in" to
test the water to see if it's too hot.

Here we go loop de loo,
Here we go loop de la,
Here we go loop de loo,
All on a Saturday night.

You put your right hand in,
You put your right hand out,
You give your right hand a shake, shake, shake,
And turn yourself about.

The song can be found on several recordings. My favorite versions include *We All Live Together, Vol. 1,* by Greg and Steve and *Shake It to the One That You Love the Best: Play Songs and Lullabies from Black Musical Traditions* by Cheryl Warren Mattox.

Mix and Match

ADDITIONAL PICTURE BOOKS

Kudrna, C. Imbrior. *To Bathe a Boa.*

> Even snakes need baths. There are wonderful illustrations of the boa house (a long, curvy version of a dog house) and of the boa hiding behind glasses with a fake nose.

Munsch, Robert. *Mud Puddle.*

> Every time a girl walks outside, a mud puddle jumps on her head. Munsch adds sound effects when her mother scrubs out her ears, eyes, and belly button. Add your own scrubbing "squeaks."

Pryor, Ainslie. *The Baby Blue Cat and the Dirty Dog Brothers.*

> The cats and dogs play in a mud puddle, get cleaned up, receive snacks, then hop back in the mud puddle to eat the snacks.

Watanabe, Shigeo. *I Can Take a Bath.*

> Little Bear joins his Daddy in the tub. The adults and children in the audience can take turns "scrubbing" each other's backs.

Zion, Gene. *Harry the Dirty Dog.*

> Here's the classic story of a white dog with black spots who gets so dirty that his family doesn't recognize him.

ADDITIONAL POEMS

"Bertie Bertie" by Eve Merriam from *Blackberry Ink.*

"Clean Gene" by Shel Silverstein from *Falling Up.*

"Dainty Dottie Dee" by Jack Prelutsky from *The New Kid on the Block.*

"The Muddy Puddle" by Dennis Lee from *Garbage Delight.*

"The Way They Scrub" by A. B. Ross from *Read Aloud Rhymes for the Very Young,* edited by Jack Prelutsky.

"Trips" by Nikki Giovanni from *Spin a Soft Black Song.*

ADDITIONAL SONGS AND MUSICAL ACTIVITIES

"Bathtime" by Raffi from *Everything Grows.*

"I Love Mud" by Rick Charette from *Alligator in the Elevator.*

"Rubber Blubber Whale" by John McCutcheon from *Howjadoo.*

"Singing in the Tub" by The Chenille Sisters on *1-2-3 for Kids.*

"There's a Hippo in My Tub" by Joanie Bartels from *Bathtime Magic.*

ADDITIONAL FINGERPLAYS AND MOVEMENT ACTIVITIES

"Bubble Bath"
Rob Reid

> Bubbly, bubbly bubble bath,
> > *(Wiggle all ten fingers)*
> Filled to the top,
> > *(Raise fingers overhead)*
> Listen to the bubbly bubbles,
> > *(Cup hand to ear)*
> Pop! Pop! Pop!
> > *(Clap three times)*

"The Old Woman"
traditional

> The old woman stands at the tub, tub, tub,
> > *(Hold up pointer finger)*
> The dirty clothes to rub, rub, rub.
> > *(Rub hands together)*
> But when they are clean and fit to be seen,
> > *(Hold up imaginary clothes)*
> She'll dress like a lady and dance on the green.
> > *("Dance" pointer finger)*

VIDEOS

Harry the Dirty Dog. Weston Woods. (9 min.)

King Bidgood's in the Bathtub. Random House. (8 min.)

Let's Give Kitty a Bath. Phoenix Films. (12 min.)

The Piggy in the Puddle. Reading Rainbow. (5 min.)

Creepy Crawlers

Program at a Glance

MUSIC	"My Brother Eats Bugs" from *See Ya Later, Alligator* by Hans Mayer
RIDDLES	"Insect Riddles" from *Going Buggy* by Peter and Connie Roop and *Buggy Riddles* by Kate McMullan and Lisa Eisenberg
PICTURE BOOK	*Insects Are My Life* by Megan McDonald
PICTURE BOOK	*How Many Bugs in a Box?* by David A. Carter
PICTURE BOOK	*The Caterpillar and the Polliwog* by Jack Kent
POEM	"Dora Diller" from *The New Kid on the Block* by Jack Prelutsky
STRING STORY	"The Mosquito" from *The Story Vine* by Ann Pellowski
PICTURE BOOK	*The Very Lonely Firefly* by Eric Carle
POEM	"Glowworm" by David McCord from *An Arkful of Animals,* edited by William Cole
MUSICAL ACTIVITY	"Spider on the Floor" from *Singable Songs for the Very Young* by Raffi
MUSICAL ACTIVITY	"The Eensy Weensy Spider" adapted by Sharon, Lois and Bram from *Mainly Mother Goose*

Preparation and Presentation

As the audience enters, play the song "My Brother Eats Bugs." They will probably join in the chorus.

> There's no holes in my sweater that moths might've
>   made;
> We never buy flypaper, never need Raid.
> Come into our kitchen, you won't see a fly;
> No worms in our garden, and I'll tell you why—
>
> *Chorus:*
>   My brother eats bugs,
>   Grasshoppers, crickets, and slugs,
>   Butterfly wings, and other gross things—
>   My brother eats bugs.
>
> When we go fishing, there's one thing I hate,
> We never catch nothing, 'cause he eats the bait.
> When we have a picnic, you know what he'll do?
> If there's any ants, he'll eat them all too.
>
> *(Chorus after each verse)*
>
> He munches on hornets and never gets stung,
> But he won't eat woolly bears, they tickle his tongue.
> We caught some fireflies one night in the park,
> He swallowed them all, now he glows in the dark.
>
> Sometimes I think that my brother's part frog;
> He even eats fleas that he picks off the dog.
> But I'm starting to think that he's on the right track—
> Mosquitoes bite people, he bites them back.

When everyone is seated, tell them an insect riddle. You can find several in *Going Buggy* by Peter and Connie Roop and *Buggy Riddles* by Kate McMullan and Lisa Eisenberg. Try this one:

> What do young insects ride in?
> (Baby bug-gies)

The kids will laugh. The adults will groan. Tell everyone that they don't get any better than this. Scatter more riddles throughout the program.

Insects Are My Life
Megan McDonald

Amanda Frankenstein is crazy about insects. Amanda collects all kinds of insects; she even collects mosquito bites. This fascination leads to teasing from her brother and classmates. The story is long, but very entertaining and educational.

How Many Bugs in a Box?
David A. Carter

Weird bugs populate this inventive pop-up book. Meet fish-bugs, frog-bugs, noddle-bugs and other imaginative insects. Carter has several other bug pop-ups including *More Bugs in Boxes* and *Alpha Bugs*.

The Caterpillar and the Polliwog
Jack Kent

Several library supply catalogs carry caterpillar puppets that turn into butterflies and tadpole puppets that turn into frogs. Use the puppets after you read the book and give your audience a quiz. "Let's see, the polliwog turns into a hippopotamus, right?" Of course, the kids will shout "No!" and (hopefully) give the correct answer. It's fun to use different vocal characterizations with this particular story. Read the caterpillar's dialogue in a "snooty, high-society voice."

"Dora Diller"
Jack Prelutsky

I started reading this poem one day when the tune of "Yankee Doodle" popped out of my mouth. Try it.

"The Mosquito"
Ann Pellowski

It might take some time to learn this story's string technique, but once you know it, you'll have it forever. I usually get very quiet near the end of this story after making the mosquito string figure. Then I give a loud "SMACK" to make everyone in the audience jump. If you have a lot of infants in the audience, make a quiet "smack," or you'll have a roomful of crying kids. (I speak from experience.) After the story is over, someone invariably yells for me to do it again. I'll then perform a speeded up version of the story ("the *Reader's Digest* version for you big folks") followed by an extremely slow motion version ("slow-mo") in which my voice gets low and drawn out and the slowness of the string motions is exaggerated.

Follow this story with another riddle:

What kind of insects are good in school?
(Spelling bees)

The Very Lonely Firefly
Eric Carle

Carle designed real twinkling lights on the back inside cover to simulate several fireflies. Have someone lower the lights for maximum effect when you reach this part.

"Glowworm"
David McCord

This short, clever poem instructs you to say "Helloworm" to a glowworm, but not "What do you knowworm."

"Spider on the Floor"
Raffi

(Raffi also has a picture book by the same title.) Move the spider up your leg, stomach, face, and head during the appropriate parts of the song. Have the audience follow along using their hands and fingers to imitate a spider crawling up their bodies. If your crowd has sufficiently recovered from their mosquito scare, you can always shake things up by throwing the spider puppet into the audience while shouting "SPIDER" at the end of the song. Make sure you have a sturdy puppet because many young hands will compete to return it to you. (Again, I speak from experience.)

 ### "The Eensy Weensy Spider"
traditional, adapted by Sharon, Lois and Bram

Sharon, Lois and Bram's version can be found on their recordings *Mainly Mother Goose* and *Great Big Hits*.

   Ask everyone to stand up and help make the finger motions to "The Eensy Weensy Spider."

> The eensy weensy spider
> Climbed up the water spout.
> > *(Touch fingers together and move them upward)*
> Down came the rain
> > *(Wiggle fingers downward)*
> And washed the spider out.
> > *(Make broad, sweeping motions with hands)*
> Out came the sun
> > *(Form a circle overhead)*
> And dried up all the rain.
> And the eensy weensy spider
> Climbed up the spout again.
> > *("Climb" with fingers again)*

After performing it once, tell the crowd about the big, fat spider! Perform the traditional motions in an overly dramatic fashion. Finally, have everyone perform the motions in the miniscule manner of the teensy weensy spider in their teensy weensy voices.

   Close the session with another riddle:

> What's worse than finding a worm in your apple?
> (Finding half a worm in your apple)

Mix and Match

ADDITIONAL PICTURE BOOKS

Aylesworth, Jim. *Old Black Fly*.

A naughty fly is chased throughout the alphabet.

Carle, Eric. *The Grouchy Ladybug*.

A grouchy ladybug tries to pick fights with several animals.

———. *The Very Busy Spider*.

A spider ignores the other animals while she builds her web. Kids love to touch the raised webbing designed on the paper.

———. *The Very Hungry Caterpillar*.

One of the classic children's books concerns a tiny caterpillar with a big appetite.

———. *The Very Quiet Cricket*.

Cricket doesn't make a sound until the very last page.

Oppenheim, Joanne. *You Can't Catch Me!*

A pesky black fly irritates several animals in this story reminiscent of "The Gingerbread Man." Oppenheim's story would make a good felt story or puppet story.

Sloat, Teri. *The Thing That Bothered Farmer Brown*.

A tiny, whining insect keeps Farmer Brown and all of his animals awake. The audience will enjoy making the barnyard noises.

ADDITIONAL POEMS

"Bug" by Lois Simmie from *Kids Pick the Funniest Poems,* edited by Bruce Lansky.

"Crickets" by Aileen Fisher from *When It Comes to Bugs*.

"Fuzzy Wuzzy, Creepy Crawly" by Lillian Schultz from *Read Aloud Rhymes for the Very Young*, edited by Jack Prelutsky.

"Hurt No Living Thing" by Christina Rossetti from *Sing a Song of Popcorn*, edited by Beatrice de Regnier.

"I Want You to Meet" by David McCord from *Sing a Song of Popcorn*, edited by Beatrice de Regnier.

"The Last Cry of the Damp Fly" by Dennis Lee from *Never Take a Pig to Lunch*, edited by Stephanie Calmenson.

"My Opinion" by Monica Shannon from *Eric Carle's Animals Animals*, edited by Eric Carle.

"Raindrops" by Aileen Fisher from *Read Aloud Rhymes for the Very Young*, edited by Jack Prelutsky.

ADDITIONAL SONGS AND MUSICAL ACTIVITIES

"The Ants Go Marching" by Linda Arnold from *Sing Along Stew*.

"The Cricket Song" by Mary Lu Walker from *The Frog's Party*.

"Flea, Fly, Mosquito" by Sharon, Lois and Bram from *One Elephant*.

"Hello Ladybug" by Sally Rogers from *Piggyback Planet*.

"The Parade" by Joe Scruggs from *Ants*.

ADDITIONAL FINGERPLAYS AND MOVEMENT ACTIVITIES

"Here Is the Beehive"
traditional

> Here is the beehive,
> > *(Hold up fist)*
> Where are the bees?
> > *(Shrug shoulders)*
> Hidden away where nobody sees.
> > *(Shake fist)*

Soon they'll come buzzing out of the hive,
>   *(Peek into fist)*

One, two, three, four, five
>   *(Slowly open fingers)*

BUZZZZZ!
>   *(Flutter fingers with great speed)*

"Little Spider"
traditional

See the little spider
Climbing up the wall,
>   *(Move all fingers up arm)*

See the little spider
Stumble and fall.
>   *(Drop fingers off arm)*

See the little spider
Tumble down the street,
>   *(Move fingers on leg)*

See the little spider
Stop at my feet.
>   *(Flop fingers on shoe)*

VIDEOS

Anansi and the Moss-Covered Rock. Living Oak Media. (11 min.)

The Caterpillar and the Polliwog. Weston Woods. (7 min.)

Frogs, Snakes, Turtles, 'Gators, & Crocs

Program at a Glance

MUSIC	"The Night the Froggies Flew" from *Colleen and Uncle Squaty* by Colleen and Uncle Squaty
PICTURE BOOK	*Pondlarker* by Fred Gwynne
POEM	"The Froggy Choir" by Rob Reid
MUSICAL ACTIVITY	"Five Frogs" from *Anna Moo Crackers* by Anna Moo
FINGERPLAY	"My Turtle"
MUSICAL ACTIVITY	"You Can't Make a Turtle Come Out" from *Grandma's Patchwork Quilt*
PICTURE BOOK	*The Extraordinary Egg* by Leo Lionni
POEM	"Alligator Pie" from *Alligator Pie* by Dennis Lee
MUSIC	"Alligator Stomp" from *Anna Moo Crackers* by Anna Moo
POEM	"The Crocodile's Toothache" from *Where the Sidewalk Ends* by Shel Silverstein
PICTURE BOOK	"The Quick Slick Snake" from *Two Mice in Three Fables* by Lynn Reiser
STORY	"The Exploding Frog" adapted by Rob Reid from Aesop

Preparation and Presentation

Create construction paper frogs lying on lily pads. Fasten them on all walls and doors. A good frog pattern can be found in the book *Felt Board Fun* by Liz and Dick Wilmes.

"The Night the Froggies Flew"
Colleen and Uncle Squaty (Colleen Hannafin and
Brian Schellinger)

Play "The Night the Froggies Flew" from the recording *Colleen and Uncle Squaty* as the audience enters the story room. The song is loosely based on David Wiesner's wordless picture book *Tuesday*. Here are the first few verses of the song:

> The froggies were sleeping and it was early on,
> They were sittin' on lily pads at the bottom of the pond,
> When things started buzzin', they covered their eyes,
> And the lily pads started to rise.

> Well, they didn't have a car and they didn't really have a
>   plane,
> They had little green magic carpets and they all formed a
>   little green train,
> Then they grabbed the edge of the lily pad and they used
>   it for a steering wheel,
> And then they all took off across the field.

> Froggies on the lily pads, me oh my,
> Froggies flying across the sky,
> Flying saucers and froggies too,
> 'Twas the night the froggies flew.

Pondlarker
Fred Gwynne

A young frog behaves like a prince and goes on many adventures searching for a princess to kiss. By the end of the story, he realizes there is nothing wrong with being a frog.

Play around with the vocalizations. Read the frog's dialogue in a deep, slow voice and the princess's voice in an old, quivery manner.

"The Froggy Choir"
Rob Reid

Ask the audience "What kind of sounds do frogs make?" You'll get a variety of answers. At the end of the poem, ask the audience members to make their individual frog sound and conduct your own froggy choir.

> A froggery of frogs
> Were looking for a sound.
> They hired a frog director
> And this is what they found.
>
> He had the peepers peep high
> And the hop-toads sing low.
> The leopard frogs snarled
> (They tend to do that, you know).
>
> He taught the fat frogs how to bellow
> And the old ones how to croak.
> The baby frogs hollered
> 'Cause he gave them a poke.
>
> He made the thin frogs sing "Rib-it,"
> The horn frogs blared "Ker-dunk,"
> The mud frogs chanted "Knee-deep"
> and the rock frogs sunk.
>
> He showed the drum frogs how to rock
> And the leap frogs how to roll.
> The speckled frogs played jazz
> And the polliwogs soul.
>
> He told the tree frogs to bark
> And the cricket frogs to chirp.
> The river frogs babbled
> And the bullfrog burped.

The sound that was produced
Pleased the frog director's ears.
The beauty of their music
Simply moved those frogs to tears.

And if you have a fancy
To sing down in the mire,
You just might be invited
To join that froggy choir.

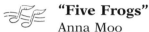

"Five Frogs"
Anna Moo

Five frogs hopping on a log,
One hopped off into the pond.
Then a big alligator came swimming along
He went "Chomp!" Mmm, Mmm.
He's gone.

(Repeat for four, three, two, and one frog)

Use the frog pattern mentioned in the introductory paragraph to make five felt froggies. Make a felt log, too. A simple brown rectangle will do. A green rectangle can simulate the alligator if you can't find a good pattern. Teach the words of this simple song to your audience, or chant it if you don't have Moo's recording. A similar song for this felt activity is "Five Little Frogs" found on Raffi's recording *Singable Songs for the Very Young.* Ask one of the children or adults to take the frogs off the felt board one by one during this backward counting song.

"My Turtle"
traditional

Ask everyone to hold up their turtles (their fists).

This is my turtle,
He lives in a shell,
He likes his home very well.

He pokes his head out,
    (Hold thumb up)
When he wants to eat,
And he pulls it back,
    (Put thumb in fist)
When he wants to sleep.

"You Can't Make a Turtle Come Out"
Malvina Reynolds

Have everyone hold up their "turtles" again for the song "You Can't Make a Turtle Come Out" from the recording *Grandma's Patchwork Quilt.* Hide the thumbs. Follow the actions of the song while you play the recording. Everyone will be knocking on the turtle's shell, shaking him, and ringing the turtle's door-bell. At the end, raise thumbs on the line "he'll be walking around with his head in the air."

The Extraordinary Egg
Leo Lionni

Three frogs find what they think is a chicken egg. When a baby alligator hatches, they all become good friends, but the frogs still think the alligator is a chicken.

"Alligator Pie"
Dennis Lee

"Alligator Pie" can also be found in *The Random House Book of Poetry for Children,* edited by Jack Prelutsky.

    This poem always gets a smile. It's easy to make up your own verses. Here's one I wrote by following the pattern of Lee's poem.

Alligator spaghetti, alligator spaghetti,
If I don't get some, I'm gonna throw confetti.
Give away my Barbie doll, give away my teddy,
But don't give away my alligator spaghetti.

"Alligator Stomp"
Anna Moo

Play Moo's recording. The audience will join in on the chorus.

Chorus:
>He do the alligator stomp,
>Stomp! Stomp!
>In the Florida swamp,
>Swamp! Swamp!
>And his jaw goes chomp,
>Chomp! Chomp!
>And his tail goes thomp,
>Thomp! Thomp!
>He dances all night long
>To that crazy song.

"The Crocodile's Toothache"
Shel Silverstein

Demonstrate what *could* happen between a crocodile and a dentist with this Silverstein poem. Use puppets if you have them. If the crocodile puppet has a huge, movable mouth, snap it shut when the dentist gets too mean with his pliers.

The Quick Slick Snake
Lynn Reiser

Two mice outwit a snake who tangles himself in knots. Use a snake puppet, rope, or yarn to show how the snake got "twisted and tangled and tied."

"The Exploding Frog"
Rob Reid

I tell this version of the Aesop fable with a big, green balloon. Test your balloon beforehand so you know exactly how big it will stretch. When you break the balloon at the end, hold it away from your face (it can cut your lip!) and pinch it. It will make a satisfying explosion. If you have very young children in the audience, simply let the balloon go instead of popping it, and watch it fly around the room.

Two little frogs were playing on the banks of a creek. Suddenly, a great big ox came down to get a drink.

The little frogs had never seen anything as big as that ox before. All they could talk about was the size of that ox, even after the ox left.

They talked and talked so much that they woke up a great big granddaddy bullfrog.

He listened to the little tiny frogs and said, "What you are describing is just an ordinary ox. They aren't so big. Why, if I tried hard enough, I could get as big as that ox."

The little tiny frogs said, "Oh no you couldn't."

The great big granddaddy bullfrog said "Oh yeah? Stand back and watch THIS!"

He stretched this way and that. He got bigger and bigger and bigger, just like this . . .

(Blow balloon a little bit)

"There," he said. "Was he as big as this?"

"No, no," said the little tiny frogs. "He was bigger. He was bigger."

"Bigger, huh? Okay, I can get bigger."

He stretched this way and that. He got bigger and bigger and bigger, just like this . . .

(Blow balloon bigger)

"Was he as big as this?"

"No, no, he was bigger. He was . . ."

(The audience will yell "BIGGER!")

"Bigger, huh? Okay, I can get bigger."

(Blow the balloon until it is as tight as it will get)

(In a high, tight voice)

"Was he as big as THIS?"

"No, no, he was . . ."

(Audience yells "BIGGER!")

(Start to cry)

"Okay, I can get bigger . . ."

(Hold balloon away from your face and "explode the frog")

BOOM!

The little tiny frogs picked up what was left of the great big granddaddy bullfrog.

(Pick up balloon pieces)

They said, "He was ALMOST as big as that ox . . . but not quite big enough."

And that's the story of "The Exploding Frog."

Mix and Match

ADDITIONAL PICTURE BOOKS

Ata, Te. *Baby Rattlesnake.*

Baby Rattlesnake plays tricks with his new rattle in this Chickasaw legend.

Hadithi, Mwenye. *Crafty Chameleon.*

Chameleon gets fed up with Leopard and Crocodile's bullying antics.

Johnson, Angela. *The Girl Who Wore Snakes.*

A girl who lets her pet snakes crawl on her is delighted to find a relative who also is fond of snakes.

Lionni, Leo. *Cornelius.*

Cornelius the crocodile proves to be different from the other crocodiles by walking upright, standing on his head, and hanging from trees by his tail.

Sadler, Marilyn. *Elizabeth and Larry.*

A middle-aged woman leads a comfortable, yet silly, life with her companion Larry, an alligator.

Sierra, Judy. *Counting Crocodiles.*

A monkey who lives in the middle of the Sillabobble Sea tricks the Sillabobble crocodiles.

Stevens, Janet. *The Tortoise and the Hare.*

Rabbit has several funny lines in this retelling of the Aesop fable, including "Slow down, you bowlegged reptile!"

ADDITIONAL POEMS

"The Alligator" by Mary MacDonald from *The Random House Book of Poetry for Children,* edited by Jack Prelutsky.

"As I Was Walking Round the Lake" from *Poems of A. Nonny Mouse,* edited by Jack Prelutsky.

"Frog" by Mary Ann Hoberman from *Yellow Butter, Purple Jelly, Red Jam, Black Bread.*

"The Frog on the Log" by Ilo Orleans from *Read Aloud Rhymes for the Very Young,* edited by Jack Prelutsky.

ADDITIONAL SONGS AND
MUSICAL ACTIVITIES

"Boa Constrictor" by Peter, Paul and Mary from *Peter, Paul and Mommy.*

"The Foolish Frog" by Pete Seeger from S*tories and Songs for Little Children.*

"I'm Being Swallowed by a Boa Constrictor" by The Chenille Sisters from *1-2-3 for Kids.*

"Newts, Salamanders and Frogs" by Banana Slug String Band from *Dirt Made My Lunch.*

"Susie and the Alligator" by Cathy Fink and Marcy Marxer from *A Cathy and Marcy Collection for Kids.*

ADDITIONAL FINGERPLAYS AND
MOVEMENT ACTIVITIES

"I'm a Little Toad"
traditional

> I'm a little toad
> Hopping down the road,
> > *(Make fingers hop)*
> Listen to my song,
> I sleep all winter long.
> > *(Pretend to sleep)*
> When spring comes, I peek out
> > *(Peek from behind hands)*

And then I jump about,
>   *(Jump)*
And now I catch a fly,
>   *(Clap)*
And now I wink my eye,
>   *(Wink)*
And now and then I hop,
>   *(Hop)*
And then I finally stop.

"This Is My Turtle"
traditional

This is my turtle,
>   *(Make a fist)*
She lives in a shell.
>   *(Hide thumb)*
She likes her home
Very well.

She pokes her head out,
>   *(Show thumb)*
When she wants to eat,
And pulls it back
>   *(Hide thumb)*
When she wants to sleep.

VIDEOS

Anansi Goes Fishing. Living Oak Media. (11 min.)

Frog and Toad Together. Churchill Media. (14 min.)

Frog Goes to Dinner. Phoenix Films. (12 min.)

Jammy Jamboree

Program at a Glance

MUSIC	*Good Times and Bed Times* by Si Kahn
POEM	"You've No Need to Light a Night Light"
PICTURE BOOK	*Two Terrible Frights* by Jim Aylesworth
PICTURE BOOK	*The Napping House* by Audrey Wood
PICTURE BOOK	*Nathaniel Willy, Scared Silly* by Judith Matthews and Fay Robinson
MUSICAL ACTIVITY	"Whole Bed" adapted by Joe Scruggs from *Bahamas Pajamas*
PICTURE BOOK	*Wake Up, Wake Up* by Brian and Rebecca Wildsmith
PICTURE BOOK	*Peace at Last* by Jill Murphy
POEM	"Things to Do if You Are a Star" by Bobbi Katz from *Go to Bed: A Book of Bedtime Poems,* edited by Lee Bennett Hopkins
MUSIC	"Twinkle, Twinkle, Little Star"
FINGERPLAY	"Sleepy Fingers"
POEM	"Keep a Poem in Your Pocket" by Beatrice Schenk de Regnier from *The Random House Book of Poetry for Children,* edited by Jack Prelutsky
MUSIC	Selection from *Stardreamer* by Priscilla Herdman

Preparation and Presentation

Post announcements inviting all children to attend a "Jammy Jamboree" party in their pajamas with their favorite stuffed animal. (We've even had a few parents show up in their robes, slippers, and flannel long johns.) Show up in your own night outfit. I have a flannel nightshirt and oversized wolf slippers that howl.

Play selections from the recording *Good Times and Bed Times* by Si Kahn as the audience enters the story area.

"Settle down for some bedtime stories. Imagine we're cuddling in our blankets and afghans . . . the moon is out . . . the night light is on. . . . Wait a minute! Do we really need a night light?"

At this point, I remove a night light I had placed earlier in the wall outlet and recite the following traditional, tongue-twisting poem.

"You've No Need to Light a Night Light"
anonymous

> You've no need to light a night light on a light night like
>   tonight.
> For a night light's light's a slight light while tonight's a
>   night that's light.
> When a night's light, like tonight's light, it's really not
>   quite right
> To light night lights with their slight lights on a light
>   night like tonight.

It's a challenge to read this poem, let alone memorize it. But your audience will appreciate your effort. When you've finished, fan your "overheated" tongue while the audience breaks into applause.

Two Terrible Frights
Jim Aylesworth

A little girl and a little mouse frighten each other at night. The audience usually laughs when the mouse tells its mother that the girl "eeked" at it while the girl tells her mother that the mouse "squeaked" at her.

The Napping House
Audrey Wood

This is one of my favorite illustrated books (beautifully drawn by the author's husband Don Wood). A boy, a dog, a cat, and a mouse join the snoring granny "on a cozy bed in a napping house where everyone is sleeping" moments before a wakeful flea bites the mouse and starts a wakeful chain of events.

Nathaniel Willy, Scared Silly
Judith Matthews and Fay Robinson

This is a highly participative retelling of the folk tale "The Squeaky Door." There are several repetitive lines that the audience will quickly learn and recite during the course of the story. The audience will also have a chance to make a lot of kissy noises and the loudest, most ear-splitting door squeak in the history of your library. ("Didn't you always want to do that in a library?") This is a story I like to tell without the book. Encourage the parents to check the book out and share the wonderful illustrations (such as the grandma carrying the cow and the pig) with their children at home.

"Whole Bed"
adapted by Joe Scruggs

Scruggs has created a new ending for the traditional song "Ten in a Bed." After singing the final verse "There were two in the bed and the little one said 'Roll Over,'" Scruggs starts singing "I've got the whole bed to myself" to the tune of "He's Got the Whole World in His Hands." Sharon, Lois and Bram give a similar treatment of the song on their recording *The Elephant Show Record*. Here are the words to the traditional "Ten in a Bed."

> There were ten in a bed and the little one said, "Roll over, roll over."
> So they all rolled over and one fell out,

There were nine in the bed and the little one said,
"Roll over, roll over."
So they all rolled over and one fell out . . .
   (Continue down to one)

Wake Up, Wake Up
Brian and Rebecca Wildsmith

This picture book can be effectively turned into a felt board story. The sun wakes up the rooster who wakes up the goose who wakes up the sheep and the goat and the pig and the cow until the farmer in turn feeds the cow, the pig, the goat, and so on. Look for felt patterns of most of the animals in Liz and Dick Wilmes's book *Felt Board Fun*.

Peace at Last
Jill Murphy

Mr. Bear can't sleep because of Mrs. Bear's snoring, the clock's loud tick-tocking, the faucet dripping, and the owl's hooting. The audience can help make the sound effects, especially the alarm clock that rings just as Mr. Bear falls asleep.

"Things to Do if You Are a Star"
Bobbi Katz

Here is a very short ditty that responds to the poem's title by twinkling and twinkling.

"Twinkle, Twinkle, Little Star"
traditional

With all of the "twinkles" mentioned in the above poem, a good follow-up would be a family sing-along of this popular nursery rhyme.

Twinkle, twinkle, little star,
How I wonder what you are,

Up above the world so high,
Like a diamond in the sky,
Twinkle, twinkle, little star,
How I wonder what you are.

"Sleepy Fingers"
traditional

My fingers are so sleepy
(Hold up five fingers on one hand)
It's time they went to bed.
First you, Baby Finger,
*(One by one fold your fingers down, parents can help
the little ones hold their fingers down)*
Tuck in your little head.
Ring Man, now it's your turn.
Then comes Tall Man great,
Pointer Finger, hurry,
'cause it's getting late.
Let's see if they're all nestled.
No, there's one to come.
Move over, little Pointer,
Make room for Master Thumb.
(Lay your head on your hands)

"Keep a Poem in Your Pocket"
Beatrice Schenk de Regniers

Close the program by reciting Beatrice Schenk de Regnier's poem about keeping a poem in your head "at night when you're in bed."

Play a lullaby recording as the audience files out. My favorites are the Earth Mother recordings by Pamela Ballingham, *Stardreamer* by Priscilla Herdman, *40 Winks* by Jessica Harper, *Dedicated to the One I Love* by Linda Ronstadt, and *All through the Night* by Mae Robertson and Don Jackson.

Mix and Match

ADDITIONAL PICTURE BOOKS

Alda, Arlene. *Sheep, Sheep, Sheep, Help Me Fall Asleep.*
Instead of counting sheep to fall asleep, a child counts cows, cats, pigs, gorillas, and other animals.

Brown, Margaret Wise. *Little Donkey, Close Your Eyes.*
Different animals and a child are encouraged by their parents to slow down and get ready for a good night's sleep.

Carlstrom, Nancy White. *Northern Lullaby.*
Incredible illustrations by Leo and Diane Dillon highlight these "goodnights" to the natural entities of Alaska.

Edwards, Richard. *Something's Coming!*
Three little toys are sure that something is coming in the middle of the night and it finally does—a sneeze.

Knutson, Kimberley. *Bed Bouncers.*
A brother and sister are expert bed bouncers who bounce so high that they bounce into outer space where they meet bed bouncers of all races and nations.

Mwalimu and Adrienne Kennaway. *Awful Aardvaark.*
Aardvaark's snoring keeps the other animals awake in this "pourquoi" story of why Aardvaark eats termites at night.

ADDITIONAL POEMS

"Bedtime" by Eleanor Farjeon from *Go to Bed: A Book of Bedtime Poems,* edited by Lee Bennett Hopkins.

"Hushabye My Darling" by Clyde Watson from *When the Dark Comes Dancing: A Bedtime Poetry Book,* edited by Nancy Larrick.

"I'm Much Too Tired to Play Tonight" by Jack Prelutsky from *Something Big Has Been Here.*

"Moonstruck" by Aileen Fisher from *Still as a Star: A Book of Nighttime Poems,* edited by Lee Bennett Hopkins.

"Night Warning" by Babs Bell Hajdusiewicz from *A Bad Case of the Giggles,* edited by Bruce Lansky.

"Song to Straighten a Bad Dream" by John Bierhorst from *On the Road of Stars: Native American Night Poems and Sleep Charms.*

"Tucking-In Song" from *Songs from Dreamland* by Lois Duncan.

"You Be Saucer, I'll Be Cup" by Eve Merriam from *You Be Good and I'll Be Night.*

ADDITIONAL SONGS AND MUSICAL ACTIVITIES

"The Bear That Snores" by Kevin Roth from *Travel Song Sing Alongs* and *Unbearable Bears.*

"Bedtime Round" by Tom Chapin from *Billy the Squid.*

"It's Time to Go to Bed" by Rick Charette from *Chickens on Vacation.*

"Sleep, Sleep" by Rosenshontz from *Share It.*

"Time to Sleep" by Marcy Marxer from *Jump Children.*

"Where's My Pajamas" by Pete Seeger from *Abiyoyo and Other Story Songs for Children.*

ADDITIONAL FINGERPLAYS AND MOVEMENT ACTIVITIES

"Busy Day"
Rob Reid

> Here they are—
> My family and friends;
> > *(Hold up five fingers)*
> They had a busy day.
> > *(Wiggle fingers)*

Now they all
Are going to bed
> *(Bend fingers down)*

And this is what they say:
"Shhhh . . ."
> *(Finger to lips)*

"Rock-a-Bye Baby"

traditional

Rock-a-bye baby
> *(Everyone stands; fold arms and rock)*

On the treetop.
When the wind blows
> *(Move arm for wind)*

The cradle will rock.
When the bough breaks
> *(Point upward in horror)*

The cradle will fall,
And down will come baby,
> *(Pretend to catch the baby)*

Cradle and all.

VIDEOS

Ira Sleeps Over. Phoenix Films. (17 min.)

The Napping House. Weston Woods. (5 min.)

Meow & Squeak!

Program at a Glance

POEM	"Cats" by Eleanor Farjeon from *Poems for the Very Young,* edited by Michael Rosen
POEM	"Mice" by Rose Fyleman from *Read-Aloud Rhymes for the Very Young,* edited by Jack Prelutsky
PICTURE BOOK	*Chato's Kitchen* by Gary Soto
POEM	"As I Was Going to St. Ives"
POEM	"Nine Black Cats" from *The Ice Cream Store* by Dennis Lee
PICTURE BOOK	*The Little Mouse, the Red Ripe Strawberry, and the Big Hungry Bear* by Audrey and Don Wood
FINGERPLAY	"Five Little Mice"
PICTURE BOOK	*Mouse Paint* by Ellen Stoll Walsh
FINGERPLAY	"The Quiet Mouse"
PICTURE BOOK	*Jeremy Kooloo* by Tim Mahurin
MUSICAL ACTIVITY	"Big Old Cat" from *Lamb Chop's Sing-Along, Play-Along* by Shari Lewis
PICTURE BOOK	*If You Give a Mouse a Cookie* by Laura Joffe Numeroff
POEM	"When I Found a Mouse in My Stew"
POEM	"There's Music in a Hammer"

Preparation and Presentation

Once the audience is seated, explain that they don't need to clap after each story or poem. Instead, since the theme is cats and mice, they could either meow or squeak their appreciation. Practice meowing and squeaking.

"Cats"
Eleanor Farjeon

Use a cat puppet to help demonstrate the fact that cats can sleep on tables, chairs, and laps. This popular poem can be found in *Poems for the Very Young*, edited by Michael Rosen, and *The Random House Book of Poetry for Children*, edited by Jack Prelutsky.

"Mice"
Rose Fyleman

Follow Farjeon's "Cats" with this mouse poem using a mouse puppet. Cuddle the puppet as you conclude that "mice are nice." This poem can be found in several anthologies, including *Read Aloud Rhymes for the Very Young* and *The Random House Book of Poetry for Children*, both edited by Jack Prelutsky; *Sing a Song of Popcorn*, edited by Beatrice Schenk de Regniers; and *Mice are Nice*, edited by Nancy Larrick.

Chato's Kitchen
Gary Soto

Chato the cat invites a neighboring family of mice to dinner. Little do they realize they are to be the main course to go along with Chato's other recipes of fajitas, frijoles, salsa, and enchiladas.

"As I Was Going to St. Ives"
traditional

Family members can work out this traditional riddle together.

> As I was going to St. Ives,
> I met a man with seven wives.

Each wife had seven sacks.
Each sack had seven cats.
Each cat had seven kits:
Kits, cats, sacks, wives,
How many were going to St. Ives?

The answer: one. (The parents can quietly explain the answer to their kids while you move on to this similar poem by Dennis Lee.)

"Nine Black Cats"
Dennis Lee

Lee imitates "As I Was Going to St. Ives" with a poem about someone going to Halifax and meeting someone with several silly cats.

The Little Mouse, the Red Ripe Strawberry, and the Big Hungry Bear
Audrey and Don Wood

A mouse is tricked into sharing his strawberry with the narrator. The funniest of the bold illustrations shows the mouse trying to disguise the strawberry by placing glasses with a fake nose on it.

"Five Little Mice"
traditional

Five little mice on the pantry floor,
    (Run fingers on table top)
This little mouse peeked behind the door,
    (Wiggle thumb)
This little mouse nibbled at the cake,
    (Wiggle pointer finger)
This little mouse not a sound did make,
    (Wiggle middle finger)
This little mouse took a bite of cheese,
    (Wiggle ring finger)
This little mouse heard the kitten sneeze,
    (Wiggle little finger)

"Ah-choo," sneezed the kitten
    (Sneeze)
And "Squeak!" they cried
    (Make fingers "jump")
As they found a hole and ran inside.
    (Hide hand behind back)

Mouse Paint
Ellen Stoll Walsh

The cat can't find the white mice when they are standing on white paper. When the mice discover three jars of paint—red, yellow, blue—they have fun mixing the colors. They leave a little white paint because of the cat.

"The Quiet Mouse"
traditional

Although not necessary to make fingerplays work, I often have the audience stand up as an excuse to stretch.

Once there lived a quiet mouse
    (Hold up finger)
In a little quiet house
    (Cover finger with other hand)
When all was quiet as can be
    (Whisper this line)
OUT POPPED HE!
    (Shout the line and pull finger out from hand)

Jeremy Kooloo
Tim Mahurin

This alphabet book will only take one minute to read. The kids will enjoy the illustrations, while the adults will enjoy the clever wordplay concept of *A Big Cat*. Read the text twice. The first time, slowly turn the pages. The second around, read it quickly on the last double-page spread.

"Big Old Cat"

Shari Lewis

If you can get a copy of this Shari Lewis audio recording you will quickly learn the song "Big Old Cat." It's a call-and-response memory game with a simple melody. Start by singing "There's a big old cat out in my backyard." Add rhyming lines such as "holding a bat" and "chasing a rat" and "having a chat."

Add motions to help everyone remember the cumulative phrases (mime holding a bat, "chat" with your hand, etc.). You can easily chant the words if you don't know the melody. You can make your own variations depending on your theme. (There's a big old bear / cutting some hair / of a mare / sitting on a chair / out in my backyard.) Well, okay, you come up with a better rhyme!

If You Give a Mouse a Cookie

Laura Joffe Numeroff

I love the illustrations of this picture book, but I also like to tell the story without the book. The audience can act out the motions. Have everyone stand. Lead the actions by sweeping, cutting hair, holding up a mirror, fluffing a pillow, coloring a picture, and doing everything else the mouse does.

"When I Found a Mouse in My Stew"

anonymous

End the program the same way you began it—with two poems and your puppets. First, the mouse poem:

> When I found a mouse in my stew,
> I raised a great hullabaloo.
> "Please don't shout," the waiter said,
> "Or the rest will want one too."

"There's Music in a Hammer"
anonymous

Here's your final cat poem:

> There's music in a hammer,
> There's music in a nail,
> There's music in a kitty
> When you step upon her tail.
> Me-o-w-w-w!

And on that note, have everyone meow and squeak their good-byes.

Mix and Match

ADDITIONAL PICTURE BOOKS

Ernst, Lisa Campbell. *The Rescue of Aunt Pansy*.

A little mouse rescues a toy mouse from a cat because she thinks the toy is actually her Aunt Pansy.

Harper, Isabelle, and Barry Moser. *My Cats Nick and Nora*.

Two little girls play dress up with two cats. When the cats run away from the game, the girls entice them back with cat food and a toy mouse.

Novak, Matt. *Mouse TV*.

A family of mice argue over what to watch on television. When the TV stops working, the family discovers the joys of doing things together.

Wahl, Jan. *Cats and Robbers*.

Mrs. Mudge enlists a gang of cats to rid her house of mice. The cats quickly take over the house. When a gang of thieves arrive, Mrs. Mudge has had enough and kicks the whole kaboodle out—and invites the mice back in again.

Walsh, Ellen Stoll. *Mouse Count.*

A snake catches ten mice and places them in a jar. They escape by playing on the snake's greed.

ADDITIONAL POEMS

"Cat Bath" by Aileen Fisher from *A Zooful of Animals,* edited by William Cole.

"Cat Kisses" by Bobbi Katz from *Read-Aloud Rhymes for the Very Young,* edited by Jack Prelutsky.

"The House Mouse" by Jack Prelutsky from *Read-Aloud Rhymes for the Very Young.*

"The House of the Mouse" by Lucy Sprague Mitchell from *A Zooful of Animals,* edited by William Cole.

"I Wouldn't" by John Ciardi from *Mice Are Nice,* edited by Nancy Larrick, and *Talking Like the Rain: A First Book of Poems,* edited by X. J. Kennedy.

ADDITIONAL SONGS AND MUSICAL ACTIVITIES

"The Cat Came Back" by Fred Penner from *Collections.*

"Hickory Dickory Dock" from *Wee Sing.*

"Little Bunny Foo Foo" by Sharon, Lois and Bram from *Great Big Hits.*

"The Tailor and the Mouse" by Burl Ives from *The Little White Duck.*

"Three Little Kittens" by Sharon, Lois and Bram from *Mainly Mother Goose.*

ADDITIONAL FINGERPLAYS AND
MOVEMENT ACTIVITIES

"Five Little Kittens"
traditional

> Five little kittens all in a row,
> > *(Hold up five fingers)*
> They nod their heads just so,
> > *(Move fingers up and down)*
> They run to the left and run to the right,
> > *(Move fingers to the left and the right)*
> They stand and stretch in the bright sunlight,
> > *(Hold fingers high overhead)*
> Along comes a dog—he wants some fun,
> > *(Move thumb from other hand)*
> Meow! Watch all of the kittens run!
> > *(Hide fingers behind back)*

"Five Little Mice"
traditional

> Five little mice came out to play,
> > *(Hold up five fingers)*
> Gathering crumbs along the way.
> > *(Move fingers)*
> Out comes a kitty cat,
> > *(Move thumb from other hand)*
> Sleek and fat,
> And four little mice went scampering back.
> > *(Hold up four fingers and move them away from
> > "kitty cat")*

(Repeat with four down to one)

If the thought of having the cat catching the mice might disturb your audience, have each mouse run away behind your back.

VIDEOS

Here Comes the Cat. Weston Woods. (11 min.)

If You Give a Mouse a Cookie. Reading Rainbow.

Let's Give Kitty a Bath. Phoenix Films. (12 min.)

VIDEOS

Here Comes the Cat. Weston Woods. (11 min.)
If You Give a Mouse a Cookie. Reading Rainbow.
Let's Give Kitty a Bath. Phoenix Films. (12 min.)

Mouthsounds

Program at a Glance

MUSIC	"Sounds from A to Z" from *Share It* by Rosenshontz
MUSICAL ACTIVITY	"We Will, We Will Read Books!" by Julie Majkowski
PICTURE BOOK	*Too Quiet for These Old Bones* by Tres Seymour
PICTURE BOOK	*The Very Quiet Cricket* by Eric Carle
POEM	"House Crickets" from *Joyful Noise* by Paul Fleischman
MUSICAL ACTIVITY	"Hand Jive" from *We All Live Together, Vol. 4,* by Greg and Steve
PICTURE BOOK	*Peace at Last* by Jill Murphy
POEM	"The Crazy Traffic Light" by Rob Reid
MUSICAL ACTIVITY	"We're Going to Kentucky" from *Songs and Games for Toddlers* by Bob McGrath and Katherine Smithrim
POEM	"Clatter" by Joyce Armor

Preparation and Presentation

This program is all about sounds and making sound effects. Play Rosenshontz's "Sounds from A to Z" as the audience enters the story area.

Warn the audience that this is their chance to be noisy in the library. Tell the crowd that since everyone in the story area is expected to help with the noisy stories and songs, "We need to be sure that everyone is properly warmed up." Select a few of the sound effects that you will be using in the program, and ask the audience to repeat the noises after you give a brief demonstration. Many of the sounds they will be making can be found in the book *Mouthsounds* by Frederick Newman.

After you try a few sounds on them, teach them how to do silly claps. Teach them how to give "a round of applause" by moving their hands in a big circle while clapping. Teach them to clap with their knees, toes, elbows, and other body parts. Ask them to clap their neighbor's hands. Teach them to do the "air clap" in which they make the clapping motion but make their hands miss each other. These unusual warmups and claps will start the program off on a silly note.

 "We Will, We Will Read Books!"
Julie Majkowski

My friend and colleague Julie Majkowski took the rock group Queen's noisy anthem "We Will Rock You" from their *Greatest Hits* recording and put it smack in the library. Lead the audience in making a "stamp-stamp-clap, stamp-stamp-clap" rhythm.

> Wha'cha gonna do? Wha'cha gonna do?
> Wha'cha gonna do when the school year's through?
> Gonna hang around the place? Stuffin' your face?
> Bein' a slob and takin' up space?
> NO!
> We will, we will read books!
> We will, we will read books!

Wha'cha gonna do? Wha'cha gonna do?
Wha'cha gonna do when the school year's through?
Gonna check out a book,
Take a good look,
It's free, fast, fun, and easy to do.
SING IT!
We will, we will read books!
We will, we will read books!

Wha'cha gonna do? Wha'cha gonna do?
Wha'cha gonna do when the school year's through?
WE WILL, WE WILL READ BOOKS!

Too Quiet for These Old Bones
Tres Seymour

Granny challenges her four grandchildren to make more noise than she does.

The Very Quiet Cricket
Eric Carle

A cricket tries very hard to make a sound. The book contains a chip on the last page that simulates a cricket noise. You can make your own cricket noise from the *Mouthsounds* book. Basically, you learn to whistle backward through a mouthful of saliva. It takes a bit of practice, but it sounds very realistic once you've mastered it. I've had people look around for real crickets when I made the sound.

"House Crickets"
Paul Fleischman

Here's a chance to put some local teenagers to work. Have two teen volunteers (or anyone in the community, really) practice this poem designed for two voices. Several times during the poem, the voices simultaneously chime "crick-et." This brief presentation will demonstrate a creative way to share poetry and will be a good follow-up to the Carle book.

"Hand Jive"
Greg and Steve

Have the audience follow the rhythmic challenges of Greg and Steve's "echo" clapping activity. The rhythms get trickier as the activity progresses. Make up your own clapping rhythms. Have some of the children and parents in the audience lead their own clapping patterns.

Peace at Last
Jill Murphy

Mr. Bear can't get to sleep because of the SNORING and TICK-TOCKING and DRIP DRIPS and TOO-WHIT-TOO-WHOS that the audience will be glad to make. When Mr. Bear finally falls to sleep, his alarm clock rings.

"The Crazy Traffic Light"
Rob Reid

This poem was designed as an activity piece. Have the audience follow the movement cues.

> There's a crazy traffic light
> On a corner in our town.
> It has the normal colors,
> You know, yellow means slow down,
> And green means go
> And red means stop.
> It's all the other colors
> That'll make your mouth drop.
>
> *Chorus:*
> When you see a pink light,
> It means hop like a bunny.
> When the light is purple,
> Make a face that's funny.
> When the light turns orange,
> You should bark like a dog.
> When the brown light shines,
> You can oink like a hog.

When the white light's bright,
You should give a loud roar.
When the light turns blue,
Fall asleep and snore.

One day the workers came
To fix that crazy light.
They tried to make it like
All the other traffic lights.
They spent a lot of money
Tearing out its guts.
They tried to guarantee
Traffic wouldn't go nuts.
They put in brand new wires.
They worked all day and night.
They thought when they were finished
That they changed that traffic light.
But when they switched it on
After spending all that dough,
It flashed those crazy colors
That the kids all know.

(Chorus)

"We're Going to Kentucky"
traditional

If you have any rhythm instruments, pass them out. Maybe a local music teacher will loan some to you, or you could put some pebbles or buttons in plastic containers and tape the lids on. Otherwise, ask the parents to hand their keys over to their kids (only as impromptu instruments—not to take a spin). This song can be sung or chanted. If you have a lot of young kids, have them practice holding the instruments still. The parents can help by holding the little hands until it's time to let go.

We're going to Kentucky,
(Instruments are still)
We're going to the fair,
To see a señorita

With flowers in her hair.
> *(Start shaking instruments right after this line)*

Shake it, baby, shake it.
Shake it while you can.
Shake it like a milk shake
And pour it in a can.
> *(Mime pouring while shaking)*

Shake it to the bottom.
> *(Shake instruments next to ground)*

Shake it to the top.
> *(Shake instruments overhead)*

Shake it 'round and 'round
> *(Shake instruments while turning in a circle)*

And 'round and
Shake it 'til you STOP!
> *(Stop shaking quickly)*

 ### "Clatter"

Joyce Armor

Armor's poem is full of snores, splats, tweets, sputters, and squawks. Have fun with this cacophonous verse.

Finish the program with more unusual claps, such as a seal clap (make seal barking noises while clapping hands like flippers), cheek claps (lightly slapping one's cheeks), and eye claps (rapidly opening and shutting one's eyes). Instead of giving a "round of applause," give a "triangle of applause," a "rectangle of applause," and a "rhomboid trapezoid" of applause (shrug your shoulders and look perplexed).

Mix and Match

ADDITIONAL PICTURE BOOKS

Black, Charles C. *The Royal Nap.*

> The king stops snoring the royal snore "Aww . . . woga-oga-goga . . . oink" after Gerald, the pot scrubber, fails to get rid of his own hiccups.

Cole, Joanna. *It's Too Noisy*.

> Cole has created a nice, simple version of the popular folk tale in which a man complains about the noisy, crowded conditions in his house.

Kraus, Robert. *Musical Max*.

> Max, a blue hippo, LOVES to play any instrument he can get his hands on.

Porter, Sue. *Moose Music*.

> A moose causes problems in the woods with his screechy fiddle playing.

Shapiro, Arnold. *Mice Squeak, We Speak*.

> There are plenty of opportunities for the audience to make animal noises in this brightly colored book with pictures by Tomie DePaola.

ADDITIONAL POEMS

"The Farm Is in a Flurry" from *Poems by A. Nonny Mouse,* edited by Jack Prelutsky.

"Headphone Harold" by Shel Silverstein from *Falling Up*.

"I Speak, I Say, I Talk" by Arnold L. Shapiro from *Tomie DePaola's Book of Poems,* edited by Tomie DePaola.

"Noise Day" by Shel Silverstein from *Falling Up*.

"The Pickety Fence" by David McCord from *Side by Side: Poems to Read Together,* edited by Lee Bennett Hopkins.

"There's Music in a Hammer" from *Read-Aloud Rhymes for the Very Young,* edited by Jack Prelutsky.

ADDITIONAL SONGS AND MUSICAL ACTIVITIES

"Can You Sound Just Like Me?" by Red Grammer from *Can You Sound Just Like Me?*

"I Can Do Something I Bet You Can't Do" by Peanutbutterjam from *Incredibly Spreadable*.

"Something in My Shoe" by Raffi from *Rise and Shine.*

"This Little Song" by Shari Lewis from *Lamb Chop's Sing-Along, Play-Along.*

ADDITIONAL FINGERPLAYS AND
MOVEMENT ACTIVITIES

"Boom, Bang"
author unknown

> Boom, bang! Boom, bang!
> > *(Bang imaginary drums)*
> Rumpety, lumpety, bump!
> Zoom, zam! Zoom, zam!
> > *(Slash air with hands)*
> Clippety, clappety, clump!
> > *(Shake head side to side)*
> Rustles and bustles
> > *(Cover ears)*
> And swishes and zings!
> What wonderful noises
> > *(Throw arms up in the air)*
> A thunderstorm brings.

"Ten Galloping Horses"
traditional

> Ten galloping horses
> > *(Hold up ten fingers)*
> Came through the town.
> > *(Slap hands on legs to simulate galloping)*
> Five were white,
> > *(Hold up five fingers)*
> Five were brown.
> > *(Hold up five fingers on other hand)*
> They galloped up
> > *(Slap on thighs)*
> They galloped down.
> > *(Slap knees)*

Ten galloping horses
> *(Hold up ten fingers)*
Came through the town.
> *(Slap legs one more time)*

VIDEOS

Mama Don't Allow. Reading Rainbow.

Noisy Nora. Weston Woods. (6 min.)

The Name Game

———————— *Program at a Glance* ————————

MUSIC   "The Name Game" from the recording
                     Sillytime Magic by Joanie Bartels

PICTURE BOOK   *Chrysanthemum* by Kevin Henkes

MUSICAL ACTIVITY   "Willoughby Wallaby Woo" by Dennis
                     Lee, Larry Miyata, and Raffi from
                     Singable Songs for the Very Young by
                     Raffi

POEM   "Bernard" from *The Other Side of the
                     Door* by Jeff Moss

PICTURE BOOK   *Tikki Tikki Tembo* by Arlene Mosel

MUSICAL ACTIVITY   "Eddie Coochie" from *Dinosaur Choir*
                     by Bonnie Phipps

POEM   "Too Many Daves" from *The Sneetches
                     and Other Stories* by Dr. Seuss

FINGERPLAY   "Eye Winker, Tom Tinker, Chin
                     Chopper"

PICTURE BOOK   *Miss Bindergarten Gets Ready for
                     Kindergarten* by Joseph Slate

MUSICAL ACTIVITY   "Tommy Thumbs"

PICTURE BOOK   *Silly Sally* by Audrey Wood

FINGERPLAY   "Silly Names for My Toes"

MOVEMENT ACTIVITY   "Tony Chestnut"

Preparation and Presentation

Prepare blank name tags for everyone, young and old alike. Wear one yourself. Have plenty of markers around, and let the adults help the little ones write their names.

As people file into the story area, play the recording "The Name Game." The song can be found on the recording *Sillytime Magic* by Joanie Bartels or *The Big Picture* by The Chenille Sisters. There is a great version by Linda Tillery on the recording *Shakin' a Tailfeather* that has a nice mix of ethnic names, such as Avi, Keesha, Hector, and Raiko. If you're not as tongue-challenged as I am, you may even want to use the pattern of the song on audience member's names.

Chrysanthemum
Kevin Henkes

Chrysanthemum's classmates tease her about her name. Then they learn that their beloved teacher's real name is Delphinium.

"Willoughby Wallaby Woo"
Dennis Lee, Larry Miyata, and Raffi

Ask the children what they would do if their names were different. Sing a variation of the "Willoughby Wallaby Woo" song. Start by using your own name and the names of friends and coworkers as examples.

"Willoughby Wallaby Wob, an elephant sat on Rob."

"Willoughby Wallaby Wayne, an elephant sat on Jayne."

"Willoughby Wallaby Wavid, an elephant sat on David."

"Willoughby Wallaby Woxanne, an elephant sat on Roxanne."

Use audience names, but only if they volunteer. I've learned from hard experience that some children hate to have their names altered. Be sure to use the names of some of the adults and teens in the group. I usually end by singing "Willoughby Wallaby Wibrary, an elephant sat on the library. Yikes!"

"Bernard"
Jeff Moss

What would the world be like if everyone were named Bernard? Moss introduces us to president Bernard Washington and Bernard and the Seven Dwarfs for starters.

Ask for ideas for a similar poem. For example, "If everyone was named Daphne, you might sing 'There was a farmer had a dog and Daphne was her name-o'" or "you'd read about a little naughty monkey named Curious Daphne."

 Tikki Tikki Tembo
Arlene Mosel

I like to tell a slight variation of Mosel's story instead of reading directly from her book. I drop the references to China and set it in a nondescript land. The story isn't a true Chinese folk tale, and it offends some of my friends of Chinese heritage. The main character's full name is "Tikki Tikki Tembo-no sa rembo-chari bari ruchi-pip peri pembo." I'm always surprised how quickly the kids learn it. Tikki Tikki Tembo gets into trouble when he falls down a well and his rescuers get bogged down saying his full name to each other.

 "Eddie Coochie"
traditional

This song is tailor-made to follow Tikki Tikki Tembo. Eddie also has a long name, and he also falls into a well. Write his full name where the audience can see and chant it during the chorus.

Chorus:
> Eddie Coocha Catcha Camma Tosa Nara Tosa Noka
> Samma Camma Whacky Brown,
> He fell into the well,
> He fell into the well,
> He fell into the deep dark well.

Susie Brown, milking in the barn,
Saw him fall and ran inside to tell her mom that . . .

(Chorus)

Then old Joe, laid his plow aside,
Grabbed his cane and hobbled into town to say that . . .

(Chorus)

To the well, everybody came.
What a shame, it took so long to say his name that . . .

Eddie Coocha Catcha Camma Tosa Nara Tosa Noka
Samma Camma Whacky Brown . . .
Almost drowned!

"Too Many Daves"
Dr. Seuss

Listen for the giggles when you say the names "Sir Michael Carmichael Zutt" and "Oliver Boliver Butt."

"Eye Winker, Tom Tinker, Chin Chopper"
traditional

Scatter a series of traditional fingerplays and ditties that give new names to body parts. Start with the popular "Eye Winker, Tom Tinker, Chin Chopper." Have the adults point to the corresponding parts of the body on their children.

Eye winker
      (Point to eyes)
Tom Tinker
      (Point to head)
Nose smeller
      (Point to nose)
Mouth eater
      (Point to mouth)
Chin chopper, chin chopper,
chin chopper, chopper chin.
      (Move chin vigorously)

Miss Bindergarten Gets Ready for Kindergarten
Joseph Slate

The story shows twenty-six children, from *Adam* Knapp to Zach Blair, and their teacher Miss Bindergarten getting ready for a day of kindergarten.

"Tommy Thumbs"
traditional

Time for another activity that creates new names for body parts. Everyone hold up fingers and sing the following to the tune of "Here We Go Loop 'D Loo" found on *We All Live Together, Vol. 1,* by Greg and Steve.

1. Tommy Thumbs can sing,
   (Tap thumbs)
   Tommy Thumbs can dance,
   Tommy Thumbs go round and round
   (Turn in a circle)
   And then they clap their hands.
   (Clap)

(Continue with the following verses)

2. Peter Pointer . . .
   (pointer finger)
3. Tony Tallman . . .
   (middle finger)
4. Ruby Ring . . .
   (ring finger)
5. Billy Baby . . .
   (pinkie finger)
6. Finger Family . . .
   (all fingers)

Silly Sally
Audrey Wood

Silly Sally is as silly as her name. She walks backward and upside down. She meets several friends on the way to town. They all get stuck until Ned Buttercup rescues them.

"Silly Names for My Toes"
traditional

Here's another fingerplay that features new names for body parts. Again, have the parents point to the children's toes (and then let the kids have a turn doing it on the adults).

> Toetipe,
> > *(Point to big toe)*
> Pennywipe,
> > *(Point to second toe)*
> Tommy Thistle,
> > *(Point to third toe)*
> Jimmy Whistle,
> > *(Point to fourth toe)*
> And Baby Trippingo.
> > *(Point to last toe)*

"Tony Chestnut"
traditional

Finally, have everyone stand for "Tony Chestnut," which contains new names for several body parts. Do it three times, each time a little faster.

> To-
> > *(Point to your toe)*
> ny
> > *(Point to your knee)*
> Chest-
> > *(Point to your chest)*
> nut
> > *(Point to your head)*
> knows
> > *(Point to your nose)*
> I
> > *(Point to your eye)*
> love
> > *(Point to your heart)*
> you
> > *(Point to someone else)*

that's what
> *(Clap twice)*

To-
> *(Point to toe)*

ny
> *(Point to knee)*

knows.
> *(Point to nose)*

Here's another version my daughter Laura learned at Girl Scout camp.

To-
> *(Point to toe)*

ny
> *(Point to knee)*

Chest-
> *(Point to chest)*

nut
> *(Point to head)*

Just
> *(Point to chest)*

Got back
> *(Point to back)*

From the Army
> *(Point to arm)*

He shouldered
> *(Point to shoulders)*

His arms
> *(Point to arms)*

To face
> *(Point to face)*

Defeat
> *(Point to feet)*

Hip, hip
> *(Shake hips)*

Hooray!
> *(Thrust fist in air)*

Mix and Match

ADDITIONAL PICTURE BOOKS

Engel, Diana. *Josephina Hates Her Name.*

Josephina thinks her name is ugly and old-fashioned. Then she learns all about her namesake, a beautiful and talented great-aunt.

Galdone, Paul. *Rumpelstiltskin.*

There are several nice versions of this classic story. I'm partial to Galdone's version for read-aloud purposes. A miller's daughter tries to guess the name of the strange man who helped her spin straw into gold and now threatens to take her first-born.

Kraus, Robert. *Big Squeak, Little Squeak.*

Names don't always match their owners. Big Squeak is a little mouse who is very loud, while Little Squeak is big and quiet. They both run into trouble when they meet Mr. Kit Kat.

Lester, Helen. *A Porcupine Named Fluffy.*

Instead of calling their child Spike or Lance or Pokey (popular porcupine names), the Porcupines name him Fluffy. Fluffy becomes despondent until he meets a rhino named Hippo.

Most, Bernard. *A Dinosaur Named after Me.*

Read a few of the entries listed in the book. (The book as a whole is too long to share in a story program.) Have everyone make up new dinosaur names based on their own names. For example: Hannah-saurus, Michael-plodocus, Andy-dactyl, or Tyrannosaurus Sam.

Pringle, Laurence. *Naming the Cat.*

A family has trouble naming their new cat. Suggestions range from Kabuki and Fur Face to Orca and Vanilla Fudge.

Radunsky, Eugenia, and Vladmir Radunsky. *Yucka Drucka Droni.*

Three brothers—Yucka, Yucka-Drucka, and Yucka-Drucka-Droni, meet three sisters named Zippa, Zippa-Drippa, and Zippa-Drippa-Limpomponi.

ADDITIONAL POETRY

"Friendly Frederick Fuddlestone" by Arnold Lobel from *For Laughing Out Loud,* edited by Jack Prelutsky.

"maggie and milly and molly and may" by e. e. cummings from *The Random House Book of Poetry for Children,* edited by Jack Prelutsky.

"Peter Ping and Patrick Pong" by Dennis Lee from *The Ice Cream Store.*

"Ten Kinds" by Mary Mapes Dodge from *The Random House Book of Poetry for Children,* edited by Jack Prelutsky.

"Wally's Rhyme" by Jeff Moss from *The Other Side of the Door.*

ADDITIONAL SONGS AND
MUSICAL ACTIVITIES

"Everybody Eats When They Come to My House" by Sharon, Lois and Bram from *Elephant Party.*

"I Hate My Name" by Rick Charette from *Where Do My Sneakers Go at Night?*

"John Jacob Jingleheimer Schmidt" by Sharon, Lois and Bram from *All the Fun You Can Sing.*

"Lisa Lee Elizabeth" by Monty Harper from *Imagine That.*

"Madalina Catalina" by Bonnie Phipps from *Monsters' Holiday.*

ADDITIONAL FINGERPLAYS

"Chester"
traditional, similar to "Tony Chestnut"

Chester,
(Point to chest)
have you heard
(Point to ear)
about Harry?
(Point to hair)
He just got back
(Point to back)
from the army.
(Point to arm)
I hear
(Point to ear)
he knows
(Point to nose)
how to wear a rose.
(Make circle over chest)
Hip
(Shake hip)
Hip
(Shake other hip)
Hurray
(Fist in the air)
for the army.
(Point to arm)

VIDEOS

Chrysanthemum. Weston Woods. (13 min.)
Tikki Tikki Tembo. Weston Woods. (9 min.)

Outrageous Hats & Sensible Shoes

Program at a Glance

POEM	"Yankee Doodle"
POEM	"There Was an Old Lady Who Lived in a Shoe"
PICTURE BOOK	*Ho for a Hat!* by William Jay Smith
PICTURE BOOK	*Whose Hat?* by Margaret Miller
PICTURE BOOK	*Caps for Sale* by Esphyr Slobodkina
MUSICAL ACTIVITY	"My Hat It Has Three Corners" from *Crazy Gibberish* by Naomi Baltuck
PICTURE BOOK	*Whose Shoe?* by Margaret Miller
POEM	"My New and Squeaky Shoes"
PICTURE BOOK	*Benjamin Bigfoot* by Mary Serfozo
MUSIC	"Black Socks" from *Monsters in the Bathroom* by Bill Harley
MUSICAL ACTIVITY	"Late Last Night" from *Late Last Night* by Joe Scruggs
FINGERPLAY	"Tying My Shoe"
PICTURE BOOK	*Red Lace, Yellow Lace* by Mike Casey
MUSIC	"When My Shoes Are Loose" from *Help Yourself* by Cathy Fink and Marcy Marxer

Preparation and Presentation

Advertise that all participants should come to Family Storytime wearing a hat and something fancy on their feet. Fill the story area with lots of hats and footwear. Put them on throughout the program. Recently, I wore gold slippers, red basketball shoes, swimming flippers, a cowboy hat, a miniature firefighter hat, a baseball cap, and a beanie during the course of a Family Storytime. I also wore a nondescript felt hat into which I poked a feather for the opening poem "Yankee Doodle."

"Yankee Doodle"
traditional

Recite these two traditional rhymes. The audience will automatically recite them with you.

> Yankee Doodle went to town,
> Riding on a pony.
> Stuck a feather in his hat
> And called it macaroni.

"There Was an Old Lady Who Lived in a Shoe"
Mother Goose

> There was an old lady who lived in a shoe,
> She had so many children,
> She didn't know what to do.

Hold up a hiking boot with a paper window taped to the side and perhaps a tiny toy person or doll peeking from the top. For extra laughs, read a new treatment of the nursery rhyme by Bill Dodds from the book *A Bad Case of the Giggles*, edited by Bruce Lansky. The Dodds version ends with "the kids were all happy / but smelled like old socks."

Ho for a Hat!
William Jay Smith

This rhymed text celebrates all types of hats. Have the audience members toss their hats in the air on the last "Ho for a Hat."

Whose Hat?
Margaret Miller

This photo essay will have the children guessing who wears a pirate hat, a hard hat, a top hat, and other hats. Parents may have to help with some of the more difficult selections.

Caps for Sale
Esphyr Slobodkina

I like to act out this story instead of reading from the tiny book. Encourage the audience to shake their fists and stamp their feet just like the monkeys in the story.

"My Hat It Has Three Corners"
traditional

This song is tailor-made for a multigenerational audience. It's tough for younger children to do by themselves and even a challenge for the big people. Instruct the audience to

> point to themselves on "my,"
> their head on "hat,"
> hold up three fingers on "three,"
> and point to their elbows on "corners."

> *My hat* it has *three corners,*
> *Three corners* has *my hat.*
> And had it not *three corners,*
> It would not be *my hat.*

Recite the song slowly the first time through using the motions. The second time through the song, don't sing the word "my." Have everyone point to themselves. The third time through, don't sing "my" and "hat." Use the motions for those words. The next time, don't sing "my," "hat," or "three." Substitute the motions. On the last time around, don't sing "my," "hat," "three," or "corners." By now, some of the audience members are trying hard to keep up and giggling in the process. If you have a very coordinated audience, simply speed up the song. "My Hat It Has Three Corners" can be spoken or sung.

Whose Shoe?
Margaret Miller

Move onto the subject of shoes with a photo display of several shoes from this companion volume to Miller's *Whose Hat?* Who wears the big floppy blue and yellow shoes? How about the teeny-tiny white shoes? Again, parents and older siblings may have to help the younger children guess.

"My New and Squeaky Shoes"
anonymous, adapted by Rob Reid

Hold up a pair of clean, polished shoes as you read about the new, squeaky shoes. Instruct the audience to say "squeak-squeak" when they see those shoes. Hold up an old, beat-up pair of shoes when you read about leaky shoes. Instruct the audience to say "squish-squash" when they see this pair.

> My shoes are new and squeaky shoes,
> > *(Squeak-squeak)*
> They're very shiny, creaky shoes,
> > *(Squeak-squeak)*
> I wish I had my leaky shoes
> > *(Squish-squash)*
> That Mommy put away.
>
> I like my old brown leaky shoes
> > *(Squish-squash)*
> Much better than these creaky shoes,
> > *(Squeak-squeak)*
> These shiny, creaky, squeaky shoes
> > *(Squeak-squeak)*
> I've got to wear today.

Benjamin Bigfoot
Mary Serfozo

Little Benjamin insists on wearing his father's big old shoes to kindergarten.

"Black Socks"
traditional

> Black socks, they never need washing,
> The longer you wear them, the stronger they get,
> Sometimes I think I should change them,
> But something inside of me tells me
> Not yet, not yet, not yet.

If you like a challenge, try leading this song as a round.

 "Late Last Night"
Joe Scruggs

Play this song by Joe Scruggs. Everyone can stand up and move around the room pretending they are wearing ice skates, moccasins, tap shoes, and other types of footwear.

 "Tying My Shoe"
traditional

(*Pantomime the motions*)

> I know how to tie my shoe,
> I take the loop and poke it through,
> It's very hard to make it stay,
> Because my thumb gets in the way.

This can lead to some funny slapstick if you're the "knowledgeable" adult who gets your thumb caught in the shoestring.

 Red Lace, Yellow Lace
Mike Casey

This novelty book contains actual shoelaces and holes in the book. Use it with the fingerplay "Tying My Shoe." Invite everyone to try tying the laces of the book before leaving.

"When My Shoes Are Loose"
Cathy Fink and Marcy Marxer

As folks file out of the story area, play the recording "When My Shoes Are Loose."

Mix and Match

ADDITIONAL PICTURE BOOKS

Burton, Marilee Robin. *My Best Shoes.*

> Children wear a variety of shoes from "scuffed and muffed shoes" to "sparkling in the night shoes." The best shoes are "barefoot all day long shoes."

Emerson, Scott, and Howard Post. *The Magic Boots.*

> William's cowboy boots take him all over the world, including the Amazon Trail and the Chisholm Trail, and to the moon.

Hurwitz, Johanna. *New Shoes for Silvia.*

> Silvia receives new red shoes from Tia Rosita, but they are too big for her. She patiently waits for her feet to grow.

Nodset, Joan L. *Who Took the Farmer's Hat?*

> A farmer loses his hat to the wind and finds it converted into a bird's nest.

Stoeke, Janet Morgan. *A Hat for Minerva Louise.*

> Minerva Louise is a very silly chicken who loves to explore. She mistakes work gloves for shoes and a flower pot for a hat. She finally finds a pair of mittens to wear—one for her head and one for her tail. This is a fun story to tell with a chicken puppet.

Van Laan, Nancy. *This Is the Hat.*

> This is similar to Nodset's book about the farmer's hat. A man loses his hat to the wind and it is used as a spider's house, a mouse's bed, a scarecrow, a bird's nest, and more.

There are a lot of sound effect possibilities throughout this rhymed text.

ADDITIONAL POEMS

"Aunt Samantha" by Jack Prelutsky from *The Queen of Eene.*

"A Closet Full of Shoes" by Shel Silverstein from *Falling Up.*

"Lost Cat" by Shel Silverstein from *A Light in the Attic.*

"Mistress Pat" by Arnold Lobel from *Whiskers and Rhymes.*

"Stinky Feet" by Shirlee Curlee Bingham from *A Bad Case of the Giggles,* edited by Bruce Lansky.

ADDITIONAL SONGS AND MUSICAL ACTIVITIES

"The Best Old Hat" by Peanutbutterjam from *Simply Singable.*

"Happy Feet" by Fred Penner from *Happy Feet.*

"Sneakers" by Tickle Tune Typhoon from *Circle Around.*

"Use Your Own Two Feet" by Marcy Marxer from *Jump Children.*

ADDITIONAL FINGERPLAYS AND MOVEMENT ACTIVITIES

"Before I Jump into Bed"
traditional

Before I jump into bed,
    (Jump)
Before I dim the light,
    (Pull imaginary overhead light chain)
I put my shoes together
    (Put two fists together)
So they can talk at night.
    ("Talk" with hands)

I'm sure they would be lonesome
If I tossed one here and there,
(Spread fists apart)
So I put them close together
(Put fists together)
For they're a friendly pair.

"Old John Muddlecombe"
traditional

Old John Muddlecombe
Lost his cap,
(Look around)
He couldn't find it anywhere,
Poor old chap.
(Shrug shoulders and look sad)
He walked down the street
(Walk in place)
And everybody said,
"Silly John Muddlecombe,
You've got it on your head!"
(Put hands on head and smile)

Oftentimes, I'll substitute one of the following fold-and-tell stories instead of a picture book:

"For Each a Hat." Kallevig, Christine Petrell. *Folding Stories: Storytelling and Origami Together as One.*

"The Rainhat." Schimmel, Nancy. *Just Enough to Make a Story.*

VIDEOS

Caps for Sale. Weston Woods. (5 min.)

The Hat. Weston Woods. (6 min.)

A Three Hat Day. Reading Rainbow.

Papas, Granddads, & Uncles

_____ *Program at a Glance* _____

MUSIC — "Don't Trick Your Dad" from *Wha'd'ya Wanna Do?* by Peter Alsop

PICTURE BOOK — *Octopus Hug* by Laurence Pringle

PICTURE BOOK — *Grandpa Toad's Secret* by Keiko Kasza

POEM — "Grandpa's Whiskers"

MUSICAL ACTIVITY — "The Marvelous Toy" from *Goin' to the Zoo* by Tom Paxton

PICTURE BOOK — *Guess How Much I Love You* by Sam McBratney

POEM — "You're My Turtle, You're My Dove" from *You Be Good and I'll Be Night* by Eve Merriam

MOVEMENT ACTIVITY — "Uncle Dave" by Rob Reid

PICTURE BOOK — *Owl Moon* by Jane Yolen

MUSICAL ACTIVITY — "Owl Moon" from *Love Is in the Middle* by Bruce O'Brien

Preparation and Presentation

Send out a special invitation for all fathers, stepfathers, grandfathers, uncles, and their families to attend this special storytime. Play "Don't Trick Your Dad" by Peter Alsop as the group joins you.

Octopus Hug
Laurence Pringle

A father plays silly, made-up games with his son and daughter. In addition to playing Octopus Hug, he also pretends to be a monster, a tree, and a riding machine.

Grandpa Toad's Secrets
Keiko Kasza

Grandpa Toad shares his secrets of survival with his grandson, but it's Little Toad who saves them from a great big monster.

"Grandpa's Whiskers"
anonymous

> Grandpa's whiskers are long and gray,
> They're always getting in the way.
> Grandma chews them in her sleep,
> Thinking they are Shredded Wheat.

This is a fun poem to read if you wear a "ZZ Top" (the rock group) kind of beard. You can make a simple beard by unraveling cotton balls and taping them to your chin.

"The Marvelous Toy"
Tom Paxton

Play a recording of Paxton's classic song. In the song, a father gives his son a strange toy that goes "ZIP when it moved / And BOP when it stopped / And WHIRR when it stood still." Teach the audience to cross their hands in a back and forth zig-zag pattern on "ZIP," lightly tap their head on "BOP," and make a circle by rolling their hands on "WHIRR." Show the pictures from Paxton's picture book while the recording plays.

Guess How Much I Love You
Sam McBratney

Little Nutbrown Hare and his father Big Nutbrown Hare share their love for each other. Follow up on this picture book love letter with the love poem:

"You're My Turtle, You're My Dove"
Eve Merriam

This is one of my favorite cuddly love poems from a parent to a child.

"Uncle Dave"
Rob Reid

Have the audience stand and repeat each line and motion in this movement activity inspired by the camp favorite "My Aunt Came Back."

LEADER:	My Uncle Dave, he likes to bowl. *(Make underhand bowling motion with right arm)*
AUDIENCE:	My Uncle Dave, he likes to bowl.
LEADER:	My Uncle Dave, he likes to fish. *(Make an overhand casting motion with left arm)*
AUDIENCE:	My Uncle Dave he likes to fish.
LEADER:	Bowl, fish. Bowl, fish. *(Alternate motions)*
AUDIENCE:	Bowl, fish. Bowl, fish.

Continue the following lines in the call-and-response manner as above.

My Uncle Dave, he likes to punt.
(Make a punting motion with right foot)
My Uncle Dave, he likes to kick.
(Make a sideways karate-type kick)
Punt, kick. Punt, kick.
(Repeat all motions in a cumulative manner)
Bowl, fish. Bowl, fish.

My Uncle Dave, he likes to twist.
(Do "The Twist")
My Uncle Dave, he likes to skip.
(Skip in a tiny circle)
Twist, skip. Twist, skip.
Punt, kick. Punt, kick.
Bowl, fish. Bowl, fish.

My Uncle Dave falls in a heap.
(Gently slump to the floor)
He's totally pooped and falls asleep.
(Place head on hands and snore)

Owl Moon
Jane Yolen

A girl shares a special time with her father searching for a great horned owl on a moonlit night. This lovely book will settle everyone down from the "My Uncle Dave" activity and get them ready for a peaceful, musical rendition of Yolen's story.

"Owl Moon"
Bruce O'Brien

O'Brien wrote this song with the blessings of Jane Yolen. Lead the audience with the following gestures while listening to the recording. Repeat the gestures as they come up in the song.

Oh, you gotta be quiet,
(Finger to lip)
Under a shining owl moon.
Under a shining owl moon.
(Make a circle overhead with arms)

Oh, you gotta be quiet,
Yes, you gotta be quiet,
Under a shining, under a shining,
Under a shining owl moon.

You gotta make your own heat,
     (Wrap arms around your body)
Under a shining owl moon.
Under a shining owl moon.
You gotta make your own heat and
You gotta be quiet, under a shining,
Under a shining, under a shining owl moon.

You gotta be brave,
     (Make a muscle)
Under a shining owl moon.
Under a shining owl moon.
You gotta be brave, gotta make your own heat,
And you gotta be quiet, under a shining,
Under a shining, under a shining owl moon.

You gotta have hope,
     (Make a circle over your heart)
Under a shining owl moon.
Under a shining owl moon.
You gotta have hope, and you gotta be brave,
Gotta make your own heat,
And you gotta be quiet, yes,
You gotta have hope, under a shining,
Under a shining, under a shining owl moon.

Mix and Match

ADDITIONAL PICTURE BOOKS

Ackerman, Karen. *Song and Dance Man.*

Grandpa leads the kids up to the attic where he demonstrates some of his vaudeville routines.

Asch, Frank. *Just Like Daddy*.

> Little bear does everything like his father—from yawning in the morning to baiting his fishing hook. However, he catches a big fish—just like Mommy.

Bunting, Eve. *A Perfect Father's Day*.

> Young Susie takes her father out for a perfect Father's Day. Coincidentally, most of the activities they do happen to be some of Susie's favorites.

Coy, John. *Night Driving*.

> A father and son take a long evening journey down the highway.

London, Jonathan. *Let's Go Froggy*.

> Froggy and his dad plan a big bike trip. (Plan on lots of action sound effects for audience participation.)

Schwartz, Amy. *Bea and Mr. Jones*.

> A kindergartner named Bea and her father switch roles. She goes to work at his office, and he becomes the best student in kindergarten.

ADDITIONAL POETRY

"Dear Hard Working Dad" by Arnold Adoff from *Love Letters*.

"Four Generations" by Mary Ann Hoberman from *Fathers, Mothers, Sisters, Brothers: A Collection of Family Poems*.

"Grandpa McWheeze" by Jack Prelutsky from *A Pizza the Size of the Sun*.

"In Daddy's Arms, I Am Tall" by Folami Abiade from *In Daddy's Arms, I Am Tall*, edited by Javaka Steptoe.

"My Uncle" by Mary Ann Hoberman from *Fathers, Mothers, Sisters, Brothers: A Collection of Family Poems*.

"Uncle Dave's Car" by Helen Ksypka from *A Bad Case of Giggles*, edited by Bruce Lansky.

ADDITIONAL SONGS AND
MUSICAL ACTIVITIES

"Be Kind to Your Parents" by Michael Feinstein from *Pure Imagination.*

"Daddy Does the Dishes" by Rosenshontz from *Family Vacation.*

"Dad's Got That Look" by John McCutcheon from *Family Garden.*

"It's My Family" by John McCutcheon from *Family Garden.*

"My Dad" by Rick Charette from *Where Do My Sneakers Go at Night?"*

ADDITIONAL FINGERPLAYS AND
MOVEMENT ACTIVITIES

"Helping Daddy"
traditional

This is a variation of the popular fingerplay "Helping Mommy."

> I help daddy,
> > *(Point to self)*
> I sweep the floor,
> > *(Sweeping motions)*
> I dust the table,
> > *(Dusting motions)*
> I run to the store,
> > *(Running in place)*
> I help him crack the eggs,
> > *(Mime cracking eggs)*
> And stir the flour for cake.
> > *(Stir)*
> Then I help him eat
> > *(Mime eating)*
> All the good things that he makes.

"Two Fine Grandpas"
traditional

This is a variation of the popular rhyme "Two Fat Gentlemen."

> Two fine grandpas met in our family's den.
> *(Hold up two thumbs)*
> Bowed most politely,
> *(Bend thumbs)*
> Bowed once again.
> *(Bend thumbs again)*
> How do you do?
> *(Bend first thumb)*
> How do you do?
> *(Bend second thumb)*
> And how do you do again and again?
> *(Bend both thumbs together)*

Repeat with other family members, uncles, brothers, sisters, aunts, cousins, etc.

VIDEOS

Always My Dad. Reading Rainbow.

Bea and Mr. Jones. Reading Rainbow.

Owl Moon. Weston Woods. (8 min.)

Super Moms (& Super Grandmas & Super Aunts)

Program at a Glance

MUSIC	"Mother's Day" from *Moonboat* by Tom Chapin
POEM	"Mom Is Wow!" by Julia Fields from *Poems for Mothers* by Myra Cohen Livingston
PICTURE BOOK	*Is Your Mama a Llama?* by Deborah Guarrino
DRAW AND TELL	*Bread and Honey* by Frank Asch
PICTURE BOOK	*Thunder Cake* by Patricia Polacco
PICTURE BOOK	*Just Grandma and Me* by Mercer Mayer
MUSICAL ACTIVITY	"My Aunt Came Back"
PICTURE BOOK	*Spence Makes Circles* by Christa Chevalier
MUSICAL ACTIVITY	"Five Little Ducks" from *Rise and Shine* by Raffi
VIDEO	"Skateboard" from the video *Joe's First Video* by Joe Scruggs
POEM	"Grandma's Lullaby" from *All Asleep* by Charlotte Pomerantz

Preparation and Presentation

Send out news releases and fliers with open invitations for all moms, grandmoms, and aunts to attend Family Storytime with their families "in their honor." As the audience enters the story area, play "Mother's Day" by Tom Chapin.

"Mom Is Wow!"
Julia Fields

This poem by Fields celebrates the "comforters of weepers," "sick-bed besiders," "lullers-abye for sleepers," and everything else mothers stand for.

Is Your Mama a Llama?
Deborah Guarrino

A llama child asks a bat, a swan, a calf, a seal, and a kangaroo if their mamas are llamas. The audience gets to call out the correct mamas based on visual clues and rhymes in the text.

Bread and Honey
Frank Asch

This story is identical to the author's out-of-print book *Monkey Face*. In this story, a bear draws a picture of his mother. On the way home from school, he meets several animal friends. Each friend makes a small addition to Bear's drawing. By the time Bear gets home, the picture doesn't look anything like his mother. Depict Bear's drawing with the silly additions on a large pad of paper as you tell the story. Artistic talent is definitely not a requirement.

Thunder Cake
Patricia Polacco

A child is afraid of thunderstorms. Her Russian grandmother helps her overcome her fear by keeping her busy baking a cake.

Just Grandma and Me
Mercer Mayer

Grandma takes the popular Little Critter to the beach. Kids today will probably recognize this story from the Living Books software game just as much as from Mayer's book series.

"My Aunt Came Back"
traditional

Have everyone stand for this popular camp favorite. Instruct them to echo each line you sing and imitate each motion. (The motions are cumulative.)

> Well, my aunt came back,
> From Timbuktu,
> And brought with her,
> A wooden shoe.
> > *(Lift and drop one foot throughout the rest of the song)*
>
> Well, my aunt came back,
> From Old Japan,
> And brought with her,
> A waving fan.
> > *(Add the motion of waving right hand)*
>
> Well, my aunt came back,
> From Old Tangiers,
> And brought with her,
> Some pinking shears.
> > *(Add scissors motion with left hand)*
>
> Well, my aunt came back,
> From Guadalupe,
> And brought with her,
> A Hula-Hoop.
> > *(Add motion of swinging hips)*
>
> Well, my aunt came back,
> From the county fair,

And brought with her,
A rocking chair.
  (Add motion of rocking forward and back)

Well, my aunt came back,
From the city zoo,
And brought with her,
Some SILLIES like you.
  (Point to the crowd)

Spence Makes Circles
Christa Chevalier

Spence gets quite messy with his art project. The audience will be able to make the same movements as Spence, such as cutting paper circles, spreading glue on the circles, getting glue on fingers, and getting glue in hair.

"Five Little Ducks"
traditional

This musical fingerplay is very popular. It can be sung or spoken.

Five little ducks went out one day
  (Hold up five fingers)
Over the hills and far away,
  (Hand over eyes as if looking far away)
Mother Duck said "Quack, quack, quack, quack!"
But only four little ducks came back.
  (Hold up four fingers)

(Repeat verses down to one little duck)

One little duck went out one day
Over the hills and far away,
Mother Duck said "Quack, quack, quack, quack!"
But none of the little ducks came back.

Sad mother duck went out one day
Over the hills and far away,
Mother Duck said "Quack, quack, quack, quack!"
And all five little ducks came back.

This is a good rhyme to act out. Ask a mom from the audience to come up with her brood. Get other young volunteers to act as the other ducks. Have the mother solo the "Quack, quack, quack, quack!"

 ### "Skateboard"
Joe Scruggs

A boy decides to give his mother a practical birthday gift—a skateboard. This four-minute music segment combines live action with funny graphics. *Joe's First Video* is one of the best children's musical videos on the market.

 ### "Grandma's Lullaby"
Charlotte Pomerantz

Charlotte Pomerantz whispers sweet terms to her grandchild, such as "sweet patootie" and "tootsie wootsie" before imploring the "little turtledove" to "hush up!"

Mix and Match

ADDITIONAL PICTURE BOOKS

Brown, Margaret Wise. *The Runaway Bunny.*
   A little bunny threatens to leave by changing into different objects. Mother bunny promises to always find him and love him.

Buckley, Helen E. *Grandmother and I.*
   Grandmother's lap is perfect for rocking and for comfort when the cat is missing and when lightning flashes.

Flack, Marjorie. *Ask Mr. Bear.*

Danny wonders what he should give his mother for her birthday. Several animals give suggestions. Danny picks Bear's suggestion—a bear hug.

Johnson, Angela. *Tell Me a Story, Mama.*

Mama tells stories about her childhood to her daughter at bedtime. The dialogue is divided into two voices. Ask a volunteer to read it aloud with you.

Wynot, Jillian. *The Mother's Day Sandwich.*

Hackett and Ivy make breakfast in bed for their mother, leaving a mess behind.

Zolotow, Charlotte. *The Quiet Mother and the Noisy Little Boy.*

Mother wishes her little boy wasn't quite so noisy. When she finally gets a moment of peace, she misses his noise. Then she meets his little friend who is twice as noisy as her son.

———. *This Quiet Lady.*

A child learns about her mother's life while looking through old photographs.

ADDITIONAL POEMS

"All Kinds of Grands" by Lucille Clifton from *Poems for Grandmothers,* edited by Myra Cohen Livingston.

"Happy Birthday, Mother Dearest" by Jack Prelutsky from *Something Big Has Been Here.*

"The Mailbox Poem" by Joanna Cole from *Ready . . . Set . . . Read—and Laugh,* edited by Joanna Cole and Stephanie Calmenson.

"Pick Up Your Room" by Mary Ann Hoberman from *Fathers, Mothers, Sisters, Brothers: A Collection of Family Poems.*

"Some Things Don't Make Any Sense at All" by Judith Viorst from *If I Were in Charge of the World.*

ADDITIONAL SONGS AND
MUSICAL ACTIVITIES

"Grandma Slid Down the Mountain" by Cathy Fink from *Grandma Slid Down the Mountain.*

"Grandma's Patchwork Quilt" from *Grandma's Patchwork Quilt.*

"I Drive My Mommy Crazy" by Gary Rosen from *Tot Rock.*

"My Mother Ran Away Today" by Barry Louis Polisar from *Family Concert.*

"Super Mom" by Eric Nagler from *Improvise with Eric Nagler.*

"What Does Your Mama Do?" by Cathy Fink from *Grandma Slid Down the Mountain.*

ADDITIONAL FINGERPLAYS AND
MOVEMENT ACTIVITIES

"Grandma's Glasses"
traditional

> Here's Grandma's glasses,
> > *(Make a circle with thumb and finger.*
> > *Hold up to eyes.)*
> Here's Grandma's hat.
> > *(Fingertips together and place on top of head)*
> This is the way
> She folds her hands
> > *(Fold hands)*
> And lays them in her lap.
> > *(Place hands in lap)*

"Mama Said"
traditional

> Mama said, "Get dressed"—1-2-3,
> > *(Clap three times 1-2-3)*
> Mama said, "Pants on"—1-2-3,
> > *(Act out the motions)*

Mama said, "Shirt on"—1-2-3,
Mama said, "Socks on"—1-2-3,
Mama said, "Shoes on"—1-2-3,
Mama said, "Sweater on"—1-2-3,
Mama said, "Time to play"—1-2-3.

VIDEOS

Blueberries for Sal. Weston Woods. (9 min.)

Joe's First Video. Educational Graphics Press, 1989. (30 min.)

Smile for Auntie. Weston Woods. (13 min.)

The Tricksters

————— *Program at a Glance* —————

PICTURE BOOK   *The Toll Bridge Troll* by Patricia
                        Rae Wolff

POEM   "The Joke"

PICTURE BOOK   *Doctor De Soto* by William Steig

RIDDLES   Guess the Nursery Rhyme

RIDDLES   Guess the Headlines

PICTURE BOOK   *Anansi and the Moss-Covered Rock*
                        by Eric Kimmel

FINGERPLAY   "Whoops Johnny"

PICTURE BOOK   *Zomo the Rabbit* by Gerald
                        McDermott

MOVEMENT ACTIVITY   "The Grand Old Duke of York"

STORY   "Sody Salleratus" adapted by
                        Rob Reid

Preparation and Presentation

This program is a good opportunity to share lots of jokes, riddles, and magic tricks. Learn at least one simple magic trick from one of the many books or videos on the market. Check out *Leading Kids to Books through Magic* by Caroline Feller Bauer. One simple trick that anyone can pull off is the "Choose an Author" trick.

Share your favorite riddles as the audience enters the story area. My favorites are:

> What's black and white and red all over?
> (A skunk with diaper rash)

> What do you get when you combine a canary with an
>   electric fan?
> (Shredded tweet)

Ask the audience for their favorite riddles to set the mood.

The Toll Bridge Troll
Patricia Rae Wolff

This is another of my favorite stories to tell. A boy outwits a troll with three riddles. After the troll fails to guess the answers to the riddles, ask the audience if they know the answers before reading the rest of the text. In the end, the troll and his mother acknowledge the importance of a good education.

"The Joke"
anonymous

> The joke you just told isn't funny one bit.
> It's pointless and dull, wholly lacking in wit.
> It's so old and stale, it's beginning to smell.
> Besides, it's the one *I* was going to tell.

Doctor De Soto
William Steig

A mouse named Doctor De Soto is a dentist who refuses to treat carnivores (with good reason). He feels pity for an ailing wolf, however, and must think of a clever way to avoid becoming the wolf's snack.

Guess the Nursery Rhyme

Read the following "high-falutin' phrases" and ask the audience for the more common nursery rhyme line. For example, when you say "A trio of myopic rodents" the audience should guess "Three blind mice." They may need an example or two before they catch on. This is a good activity for older kids and adults.

> Propel, propel, propel your flotational device.
> ("Row, row, row your boat")

> Bleat, bleat, obsidian ewe.
> ("Baa, baa, black sheep")

> Sparkle, sparkle, diminutive celestial orb.
> ("Twinkle, twinkle, little star")

> Condensed atmospheric vapor, condensed atmospheric
>   vapor, depart.
> Approach anew a differently highlighted axis rotation.
> ("Rain, rain, go away. Come again another day.")

Popular contemporary titles also work. "The Feline in the Headgear" will bring about shouts of *The Cat in the Hat*. "Departure with the Natural Movement of Air" might be guessed by older audience members as *Gone with the Wind*. Ask the audience for their own examples, or have them challenge you by repeating another nursery rhyme or popular phrase or title, and see if you can substitute "high-falutin' words" for the ordinary words. (Be sure to have a dictionary or thesaurus handy!)

Guess the Headlines

Here's another variation of riddle activities. Ask the audience to guess what story or poem is described in these "headlines."

Youngster Vanishes in a Freak Wild Storm
(*The Wizard of Oz*)

Mechanically Inclined Porker Outwits Sly Adversary
("The Three Pigs")

Unique Individual Mortally Injured in Fall
("Humpty Dumpty")

Remote Country Home Vandalized by Blonde
("Goldilocks and the Three Bears")

Friendless Waif Adopted by Group of Miners
("Snow White and the Seven Dwarfs")

Continued Prevarication Elongates Proboscis
(*Pinocchio*)

Couple Suffering Dietary Allergies Reach Agreement
("Jack Sprat")

Musical Feline, Amused Canine Witness Lunar Leap
("Hey Diddle Diddle")

Rural Homemaker Terrorized by Sightless Rodents
("Three Blind Mice")

Elderly Housewife and Canine Pet Face Starvation
("Old Mother Hubbard")

Anansi and the Moss-Covered Rock
Eric Kimmel

Anansi the trickster uses the magical powers of a special rock to steal the animals' food. I like to tell this story with paper plate puppets in the shapes of the spider, the lion, the elephant, and the deer. I also "faint" at the end of the story when I say the title, much like the book characters who faint when they say the phrase "moss-covered rock."

"Whoops Johnny"

Have everyone hold out a hand, fingers spread wide.

Johnny
> *(Point to little finger)*

Johnny
> *(Point to ring finger)*

Johnny
> *(Point to middle finger)*

Johnny
> *(Point to pointer finger)*

Whoops
> *(Slide finger from pointer finger to thumb)*

Johnny
> *(Point to thumb)*

Whoops
> *(Slide finger from thumb to pointer finger)*

Johnny
> *(Point to pointer finger)*

Johnny
> *(Point to middle finger)*

Johnny
> *(Point to ring finger)*

Johnny
> *(Point to pinkie finger)*

The trick is to point to the correct finger at the right time as you repeat these steps faster and faster.

Zomo the Rabbit
Gerald McDermott

Zomo tries to earn wisdom by performing three impossible tasks. He must bring back the scales of Big Fish in the sea, the milk of Wild Cow, and the tooth of Leopard.

"The Grand Old Duke of York"
traditional

The first time through, move slowly. Repeat it faster and faster until everyone giggles so hard, they can't continue.

The Grand Old Duke of York,
He had ten thousand men.
He marched them up a hill,
> *(Everyone stands)*

He marched them down again.
> *(Everyone sits)*

And when they're up, they're up,
> *(Everyone stands)*

And when they're down, they're down.
> *(Everyone sits)*

But when they're only halfway up,
> *(Everyone crouches)*

They're neither up
> *(Everyone stands)*

Nor down.
> *(Everyone sits)*

"Sody Salleratus"
adapted by Rob Reid

There are several picture book versions of this popular Appalachian story, but I like to tell the story while audience members act out the parts. Ask for volunteers. You will need a man to play the grandfather, a woman to play the grandmother, a boy to play their grandson, a girl to play their granddaughter, someone of any age to play the pet squirrel, someone to play a storekeeper, and a small, but loud, child to play the bear. I tell the audience they need to sing the title phrase "Sody, Sody, Sody Salleratus" over and over (to any tune you make up on the spot). The audience should also turn their arms and hands into bear jaws, clap, and say "GULP!" each time the narrator says "The bear swallowed him whole."

There once was a man and a woman who lived in a cabin in the woods with their grandson, their granddaughter, and their pet squirrel. Everyone wave to the audience. *(The characters wave.)*

One day the grandmother wanted to bake some biscuits, but she was out of sody salleratus. That's an old-fashioned term for baking soda. She gave her grandson a nickel and told him to head down to the store and buy some sody salleratus.

He skipped along singing *(direct the audience to sing)* "Sody, sody, sody salleratus."

He entered the store and bought a can of sody salleratus from the storekeeper. Then he said that he thought he'd head home by way of the shortcut.

As soon as he left the store, a bear jumped out and growled. *(Instruct the bear to growl.)* The bear said, "I'm going to swallow you and your can of sody salleratus" and the bear swallowed him whole. *(The audience claps and shouts "GULP!" Instruct the boy to stand behind the bear.)*

The grandmother told her granddaughter to go down to the store to see what was keeping the little boy.

The girl skipped down the path singing *(audience)* "Sody, sody, sody salleratus."

She got to the store and asked if her little brother had been there. The storekeeper nodded her head *(help the storekeeper nod vigorously)* and said that he went home by way of the shortcut. The little girl thanked her and headed out of the store.

As soon as she left the store, a bear jumped out and growled. "I swallowed a little boy and his can of sody salleratus and I'm going to swallow you, too." And the bear swallowed her whole. *(Audience claps and gulps. The girl stands in line behind the boy.)*

The grandmother told her husband to head down to the store and see what's keeping those grandkids of his.

The old man hobbled down the path singing *(audience)* "Sody, sody, sody salleratus."

He got to the store and asked the storekeeper if she had seen his grandkids. The storekeeper nodded her head *(nod storekeeper's head)* and told him they went home by way of the shortcut.

He left the store, and the bear jumped out and growled *(bear growls)*. "I swallowed a boy and his can of sody salleratus and a little girl and I'm gonna swallow you, too." And the bear swallowed him whole. *(Audience claps and gulps. The grandfather stands in line behind the kids.)*

The grandmother threw up her arms and said "I guess I have to do everything myself." She wobbled down the path singing *(audience)* "Sody, sody, sody salleratus."

She saw the storekeeper and asked if she had seen her family. The storekeeper nodded her head *(nod storekeeper's head)* and told her they all went home by way of the shortcut.

The grandmother left the store. The bear jumped out and growled *(bear growls)*. "I swallowed a little boy and his can of sody salleratus, a little girl, an old man, and I'm going to swallow you, too." And the bear swallowed her whole. *(Audience claps and growls. The grandmother gets in line.)*

Meanwhile, who was back at the cabin? Right, the pet squirrel!

The squirrel scampered down the path singing "'Chirp, chirp, chirp, chirp, chirp-chi-chirp-chi-chirp-chirp."

The squirrel hopped onto the storekeeper's counter and asked "Chirp? Chirp, chirp, chirp?"

The storekeeper nodded *(nod storekeeper's head)* and said, "Yep, they was all here. Went home by way of the shortcut."

The squirrel hopped down from the counter and headed out the door. The bear jumped out and growled. *(Bear growls.)* "I swallowed a little boy and his can of sody salleratus, a little girl, an old man, and an old woman, and I'm going to swallow you, too."

BUT, before the bear could swallow the squirrel, the squirrel scampered up a tree. *(Instruct the squirrel to pretend to climb.)*

The bear said, "If you could scamper up a tree, I could, too." *(The bear pretends to climb.)*

The squirrel crawled out onto a branch. *(Squirrel pretends to crawl.)*

The bear said, "If you can crawl onto a branch, I could, too." *(Bear pretends to crawl.)*

Then the squirrel leaped from one tree to another. *(Squirrel pretends to leap.)*

The bear said, "If you can leap from one tree to another, I could, too."

But the bear couldn't make it the whole way. Down the bear went and landed with a SPLAT. *(Bear falls to the ground.)* And OUT of the bear's mouth popped the little boy and his can of sody salleratus, the little girl, the grandfather, and the grandmother. *(The actors return to their original positions.)* The grandmother turned around, shut the bear's mouth, gave it a swat on the behind, and told it to stay in the deep woods.

They all went home where the grandmother made a big batch of biscuits with the sody salleratus. They invited the storekeeper over. The little boy ate two biscuits, the little girl ate three biscuits, the grandfather ate four biscuits, the grandmother ate five biscuits, the storekeeper ate six biscuits, and the little squirrel ate four hundred and ninety-eight biscuits. And that's the story of *(everyone sings)* "Sody, sody, sody salleratus." Everyone take a bow!

Mix and Match

ADDITIONAL PICTURE BOOKS

Aardema, Verna. *Who's in Rabbit's House?*

The animals hear the sound of a big, bad voice from within Rabbit's house. The voice threatens to trample them. The big, bad voice turns out to belong to Caterpillar.

Goble, Paul. *Iktomi and the Boulder.*

> Vain Iktomi is pinned by a gigantic boulder. He tricks the bats into saving him.
>
> Invite two teens or adults to read one of the three voices Goble adds to his Iktomi books. One voice is identified by bold type, another by gray type, and the third by small type.

Kesey, Ken. *Little Tricker the Squirrel Meets Big Double the Bear.*

> This long story describes Little Tricker's encounter with Big Double who yells "I'm DOUBLE BIG and I'm DOUBLE BAD and I'm DOUBLE DOUBLE HONNNGRY!"

McDermott, Gerald. *Coyote.*

> Blue Coyote asks the crows to teach him to fly. This tale from the people of the Pueblo of Zuni explains why Coyote is now the color of dust.

Stevens, Janet. *Tops and Bottoms.*

> Hare tricks lazy Bear by harvesting the best ends of the garden produce. Two-page spreads emphasize Hare's trickery.

ADDITIONAL POEMS

"Hypnotized" by Shel Silverstein from *Falling Up.*

"Oh, Have You Heard" by Shel Silverstein from *Where the Sidewalk Ends.*

"Someday Someone Will Bet That You Can't Name All Fifty States" by Judith Viorst from *Sad Underwear and other Complications.*

"Tricking" by Dennis Lee from *Alligator Pie.*

"Waiters" by Mary Ann Hoberman from *Yellow Butter, Purple Jelly, Red Jam, Black Bread.*

ADDITIONAL SONGS AND
MUSICAL ACTIVITIES

"Anansi" by Raffi from *Corner Grocery Store.*

"E, I, Addie Addie, O" by Tom Paxton from *I've Got a Yo-Yo.*

"The Freeze" by Greg and Steve from *Kids in Motion.*

"I Don't Wanna Go to School" by Barry Louis Polisar from *Teacher's Favorites.*

"Plenty of Room" by Tom Chapin from *Family Tree.*

"These Are the Questions" by Rosenshontz from *Rosenshontz Tickles You.*

"Zag Zig" by Tom Chapin from *Zag Zig.*

VIDEOS

Doctor De Soto. Weston Woods. (10 min.)

Tops and Bottoms. Weston Woods. (11 min.)

Who's in Rabbit's House? Weston Woods. (13 min.)

Uh-Oh! Accidents!

Program at a Glance

MUSIC	*Uh-Oh* by Rosenshontz
POEM	*The New Adventures of Mother Goose* by Bruce Lansky
PICTURE BOOK	*Two of Everything* by Lily Tong Hong
MUSICAL ACTIVITY	"Put Your Thumb in the Air" from *Deep in the Jungle* by Joe Scruggs
PICTURE BOOK	*Sheep in a Jeep* by Nancy Shaw
POEM	"Oh, Woe Ith Me" from *You're Invited to Bruce Lansky's Poetry Party* by Bruce Lansky
POEM	"Maxie and the Taxi" from *The Ice Cream Store* by Dennis Lee
PICTURE BOOK	*Chicka Chicka Boom Boom* by Bill Martin Jr.
POEM	"Band-Aids" from *Where the Sidewalk Ends* by Shel Silverstein
PICTURE BOOK	*Five Little Monkeys Jumping on the Bed* by Eileen Christelow
MUSICAL ACTIVITY	"Sticky Bubblegum" from *Songs and Games for Toddlers* by Bob McGrath and Katherine Smithrim

Preparation and Presentation

There are several poems and stories that can fall under the unusual category of "accidents." Play the title song from the recording *Uh-Oh* by Rosenshontz as the audience enters the program area.

If you like slapstick, you might want to open the program by taking a pretend prat-fall or stumbling about. We have a large Humpty Dumpty doll that I sit on the table. Just as I'm about to begin the program, I "accidentally" knock Humpty to the floor. I explain that we will be talking about spills, crashes, bumps, bruises, and accidents.

The New Adventures of Mother Goose
Bruce Lansky

Lansky's "fractured" treatments of Mother Goose rhymes are always well received by a mixed-age audience. Many of the poems, such as "Humpty Dumpty," "Jack and Jill," and "Jack Be Nimble" deal with unfortunate adventures. The latter finds that after jumping over the candlestick, his pants "smell just like burnt toast."

Two of Everything
Lily Tong Hong

Mr. and Mrs. Haktak find a magic pot that creates duplicates of everything placed in it. Problems start when Mrs. Haktak accidentally falls into the pot and two Mrs. Haktaks climb out.

"Put Your Thumb in the Air"
Joe Scruggs

The actions for this hilarious activity are cumulative.

1. Put your thumb in the air and you shake it all around
   Put your thumb in the air and you shake it all around
   Put your thumb in the air and you shake it all around
   Now put your thumb on top of your head . . . and
      leave it there.

(Continue with the following verses)

2. Put your tongue in the air . . . put it on your upper lip . . . and leave it there.

3. Head . . . on one of your shoulders . . . and leave it there.

4. Elbow . . . on one of your knees . . . and leave it there.

5. Foot . . . on your other knee . . . and leave it there.

The audience has now become "accidentally" twisted into human pretzels. Tell them to unwind and start once again with their thumbs. At the end of that verse, tell them to put their thumbs "anywhere you want to" and put your own thumb in your mouth.

Sheep in a Jeep
Nancy Shaw

Five sheep accidentally push their jeep into a mud puddle and then into a tree. Adults enjoy Shaw's clever wordplay, while children enjoy the action.

"Oh, Woe Ith Me"
Bruce Lansky

This poem is a good match for *Sheep in a Jeep*. The narrator loosens a tooth by crashing a bike and starts talking with a lisp. Have fun reading lines such as "I wath biking dow the thtweet."

"Maxie and the Taxi"
Dennis Lee

Here is another good poem to read after *Sheep in a Jeep*. Have the audience act out motions of driving a taxi, beeping a horn, and falling asleep.

Chicka Chicka Boom Boom
Bill Martin Jr.

This is one of my favorite books to read aloud. The words are fun to say. It is very popular, and some of your audience will no doubt chime in with their own, unsolicited "chicka chicka boom booms." The verse narrative describes the various letters of the alphabet taking a tumble from the coconut tree, including "stubbed-toe E" and "black-eyed P."

"Band-Aids"
Shel Silverstein

Since one of the letters in *Chicka Chicka Boom Boom* requires a Band-Aid, launch into Shel Silverstein's poem. Although I am loath to waste actual Band-Aids as props (the poem talks about wearing thirty-five Band-Aids), I still hold up a container of Band-Aids while reciting (and put one or two Band-Aids on my face).

Five Little Monkeys Jumping on the Bed
traditional, illustrations by Eileen Christelow

Parents will probably remember this fingerplay from their own youth. I use Christelow's picture book and have the audience act out the following motions at the same time.

> Five little monkeys jumping on the bed
>> *(Hold one hand flat and have the five fingers from your other hand "jump" on top of it)*
> One fell off and hurt his head
>> *(Hold head in hands)*
> Momma called the doctor and the doctor said
>> *(Pretend to talk on a phone)*
> "No more monkeys jumping on the bed!"
>> *(Shake finger)*

> *(Repeat with* 4-3-2-1 *and* No more monkeys jumping on the bed!*)*

The book ends with Momma Monkey jumping on the bed all by herself.

"Sticky Bubblegum"
adapted by Bob McGrath and Katherine Smithrim

I embellish the recording's version by telling the audience that I'm going to pass out imaginary Super Sticky Bubblegum. I have everyone pretend to chew a piece of Super Sticky Bubblegum. I warn them not to swallow it. They need it to play the Super Sticky Bubblegum Game. Have them take their imaginary gum out of their mouths and spread it on their hands. It'll stick to everything but their legs. Slap your legs and chant:

> Sticky, sticky, sticky bubblegum,
> bubblegum, bubblegum,
> Sticky, sticky, sticky bubblegum,
> Sticking our hands to our _____.

Have the audience name a body part: feet, eyes, head, arms, and so on. The bubblegum-covered hands get stuck securely on that area until everyone says "Unstick, pull!" Everyone's hands come free. (I jokingly ask the parents if we should leave our hands where they are when we get our mouths stuck.)

On the last go-round, I pretend that the gum accidentally stuck too hard for us to pull apart with the special words. We shout "Unstick, pull!" as loud as we can, free ourselves, roll the bubblegum into a ball, and throw it on the ceiling "where it'll stick until the next Family Storytime." (Of course, the first thing you'll hear at the next Family Storytime will be about the bubblegum on the ceiling.)

Mix and Match

ADDITIONAL PICTURE BOOKS

Birdseye, Tom. *Soap! Soap! Soap! Don't Forget the Soap!*

A boy gets into trouble when he starts repeating words he hears others say while on his way to buy some soap.

DePaola, Tomie. *Strega Nona.*

Big Anthony tries one of Strega Nona's spells and covers the entire town with a never-ending supply of cooked pasta. Strega Nona saves the day and, for punishment, makes Big Anthony eat up all of the pasta.

Rylant, Cynthia. *Henry and Mudge in Puddle Trouble.*

Read the middle story, "Puddle Trouble," in which Henry's father is upset about the mess Henry and Mudge make— upset because he wasn't invited along.

Seuss, Dr. *The Cat in the Hat.*

Here is the classic accident story about The Cat who destroys a house with the help of Thing One and Thing Two.

Shaw, Nancy. *Sheep Out to Eat.*

The five sheep are back. They enter a small tea shop and promptly smash everything after adding too much pepper to their tea and cakes.

ADDITIONAL POEMS

"I Am Falling Off a Mountain" by Jack Prelutsky from *The New Kid on the Block.*

"I Am Running in a Circle" by Jack Prelutsky from *The New Kid on the Block.*

"I Did a Nutty Somersault" by Jack Prelutsky from *A Pizza the Size of the Sun.*

"I Found a Four-Leaf Clover" by Jack Prelutsky from *The New Kid on the Block.*

"I Should Have Stayed in Bed Today" by Jack Prelutsky from *Something Big Has Been Here.*

"Who to Pet and Who Not to Pet" by X. J. Kennedy from *Surprises,* edited by Lee Bennett Hopkins.

ADDITIONAL SONGS AND
MOVEMENT ACTIVITIES

"Ants in My Pants" by Joe Scruggs from *Late Last Night.*

"Baby Bird" by Pam Beall from *Wee Sing.*

"The Ballad of Lucy Lumm" by Bonnie Phipps from *Monsters' Holiday.*

"Boom, Boom, Ain't It Great to Be Crazy" by Nancy Cassidy from *Kids' Songs 2.*

"Ebeneezer Sneezer" by Fred Penner from *Ebeneezer Sneezer.*

"Oops" by Tom Paxton from *I've Got a Yo-Yo.*

ADDITIONAL FINGERPLAYS AND
MOVEMENT ACTIVITIES

"Balloons"
traditional

> This is the way we blow our balloon.
>   *(Mime blowing up a balloon)*
> We blow!
>   *(Hold hands apart)*
> And blow!
>   *(Hold hands farther apart)*
> And blow!
>   *(Farther apart)*
> This is the way we break our balloon.
> POP!
>   *(Clap)*

"The Grasshopper"
traditional

> There was a little grasshopper
> *(Curl two fingers)*
> Always on the jump,
> *(Make the fingers "jump")*
> He never looked ahead
> *(Shake head)*
> And he got a big BUMP!
> *(Have the two fingers "crash" into the palm of the other hand)*

"The Peanut"
traditional

> A peanut sat on a railroad track,
> *(Put thumb on palm of the other hand)*
> His heart was all a-flutter.
> *(Wave hands over heart)*
> Along came the five-fifteen,
> *(Pass fist in front of body)*
> Toot! Toot!
> *(Pull imaginary train whistle)*
> Uh-oh! Peanut Butter!
> *(Cover eyes)*

VIDEOS

Chicken Little. Weston Woods. (9 min.)

Officer Buckle and Gloria. Weston Woods. (11 min.)

Strega Nona. Weston Woods. (9 min.)

Under the Deep Blue Sea, Sea, Sea

Program at a Glance

MUSIC	*Slugs at Sea* by Banana Slug String Band
POEM	"The Sea"
POEM	"When a Jolly Young Fisher"
MUSIC	"A Sailor Went to Sea" from *Wee Sing Silly Songs*
PICTURE BOOK	*Curious Clownfish* by Eric Madden
PICTURE BOOK	*My Camera: At the Aquarium* by Janet Perry Marshall
MUSIC	"Octopus" from *10 Carrot Diamond* by Charlotte Diamond
STORY	"The Klunge Maker"
PICTURE BOOK	*Baby Beluga* by Raffi
POEM	"If You Ever Meet a Whale"
PICTURE BOOK	*A House for Hermit Crab* by Eric Carle
MUSICAL ACTIVITY	"There's a Hole in the Bottom of the Sea" from *Wee Sing Silly Songs*

Preparation and Presentation

Publicize your theme and ask audience members to bring sea shells and other ocean "souvenirs." Display them on a table. Decorate the room with fish mobiles and other ocean craft ideas. Many craft books have some type of ocean patterns and decorations. Elementary kids and teen volunteers will more than likely be willing to help make them.

I like to wear hip waders and a fishing hat decorated with fish hooks for this theme. Another colleague wears a sailor hat. Play the recording *Slugs at Sea* by the Banana Slug String Band as the audience enters the story area.

Once everyone is settled, I like to start with three very short sea pieces.

"The Sea"
anonymous

> Behold the wonders of the mighty deep,
> Where crabs and lobsters learn to creep,
> And little fishes learn to swim,
> And clumsy sailors tumble in.

"When a Jolly Young Fisher"
traditional

> When a jolly young fisher named Fisher
> Went fishing for fish in a fissure,
> A fish, with a grin,
> Pulled the fisherman in.
> Now they're fishing the fissure for Fisher.

"A Sailor Went to Sea"
traditional

> A sailor went to sea, sea, sea,
> To see what he could see, see, see,
> But all that he could see, see, see,
> Was the bottom of the deep blue sea, sea, sea.

This song can also be chanted.

Curious Clownfish
Eric Madden

Clownfish leaves the protection of Anemone and explores the ocean. She meets Sea Slug, Porcupine Fish, Spottyfish, Dragonfish, Cuttlefish, and others before the scary Eel chases her back to Anemone.

My Camera: At the Aquarium
Janet Perry Marshall

The audience sees a colorful but cryptic close-up "snapshot." They try to guess the identity of the object. Turn the page to reveal the answers. They'll find a dolphin, octopus, shark, clownfish, and other aquarium inhabitants.

"Octopus"
Charlotte Diamond

Play this recording and act out the various underwater creatures as they get swallowed by bigger and bigger creatures.

"The Klunge Maker"
traditional

This silly story will delight the adults. (The kids will enjoy it, too.)

A young man enlisted in the Navy. The people in charge were trying to decide which job to assign the young man. He told them he was an expert klunge maker. Not wanting to show their ignorance about what a klunge was, they assigned him to a ship as the Master Klunge Maker.

The young man had an easy time of it. While the other sailors were busy working, he just enjoyed the ride and saw the world.

Finally, the Captain came up to him and said, "You've been on this boat for months now, and I haven't seen one klunge." (The Captain didn't want to admit that he didn't know what a klunge was, either.) "I better see a klunge in three days, or you'll be scrubbing pots and pans the rest of your stay in the Navy!"

The young man made a list of items he'd need to make a first-class klunge. The Captain had other sailors bring the items to the young man. These included nails, washers, springs, boards, pipes, gears, and all sorts of like items. At the end of the third day, the young man proudly displayed his klunge to the Captain.

All the Captain could see was a big mess of parts. He spluttered, "Well, let's see it work!"

The young man walked over to the side of the ship. He held the contraption over the edge and gave it a flip. When the big mess of parts hit the water, it made a very loud "KLLUUUNNNGGGE!"

Baby Beluga
Raffi

Show Raffi's picture book while playing the song from his recording *Baby Beluga*. I've found many audiences already know the song and are more than willing to sing along.

"If You Ever Meet a Whale"
traditional

Hold up a picture of a whale as you read or recite this short poem.

If you ever, ever, ever,
If you ever, ever, ever,
If you ever, ever, ever meet a whale,
You must never, never, never,
You must never, never, never,
You must never, never, never touch its tail.
For if you ever, ever, ever,
If you ever, ever, ever,
If you ever, ever, ever touch its tail,
You will never, never, never,
You will never, never, never,
You will never, never
Meet another whale.

A House for Hermit Crab
Eric Carle

A hermit crab finds a plain shell and decorates it with sea anemones, starfish, coral, snails, and sea urchins. This is a great story to present as a felt story or as a draw-and-tell story. Don't worry about accuracy or talent with either type of presentation. Crude felt creatures or drawings are just as effective and fun as very artistic creations. There is a hermit crab puppet on the market now. Use that with the story and decorate it with tiny shells, feathers, and other odds and ends.

"There's a Hole in the Bottom of the Sea"
traditional

I like to have the audience stand and exaggerate all motions. On the phrase "hole in the bottom of the sea," have them point downward and draw a huge circle in the air.

Their bodies will become the "log," and they should point at themselves up and down when the second verse is sung.

For "bump" on the log, have them bend an elbow.

Place a fist on the elbow to represent the "frog."

Raise a pinkie finger from the fist to represent the "wart."

Wiggle the pinkie finger to represent the "flea."

Squint at the pinkie to see the "germ."

Repeat all of these actions backward as the verses head back to the "hole in the bottom of the sea."

1. There's a hole in the bottom of the sea,
    There's a hole in the bottom of the sea,
    There's a hole, there's a hole,
    There's a hole in the bottom of the sea.

2. There's a log in the hole in the bottom of the sea,
    There's a log in the hole in the bottom of the sea,
    There's a log, there's a log,
    There's a log in the hole in the bottom of the sea.

3. There's a bump, on the log, in the hole in the bottom of the sea . . .

4. There's a frog, on the bump, on the log, in the hole in the bottom of the sea . . .

5. There's a wart, on the frog, on the bump, on the log, in the hole in the bottom of the sea . . .

6. There's a flea, on the wart, on the frog, on the bump, on the log, in the hole in the bottom of the sea . . .

7. There's a germ, on the flea, on the wart, on the frog, on the bump, on the log, in the hole in the bottom of the sea . . .

Mix and Match

ADDITIONAL PICTURE BOOKS

Cowan, Catherine. *My Life with the Wave.*

A boy brings a wave home to live with him. Eventually, the wave's mood changes (like the tide), and she becomes difficult. The boy next wonders if it would be better to bring home a cloud.

Ehlert, Lois. *Fish Eyes.*

A child imagines turning into a fish and seeing a colorful array of fish. This counting book has actual holes for the fish eyes. The number of holes on each page corresponds with the featured number.

Lionni, Leo. *Swimmy.*

A black fish named Swimmy marvels at all of the sea creatures. He eventually saves a school of red fish by teaching them to act as one giant fish.

Pfister, Marcus. *The Rainbow Fish.*

Rainbow Fish, who is full of beautiful sparkling scales, learns that he is still beautiful without the scales. This book has already become a modern-day classic.

Seuss, Dr. *McElligot's Pool.*

A boy imagines that a little farm pond is connected underground to the sea. He fantasizes catching a Dog Fish (with a collar and floppy ears), an Australian Fish (with a pouch), and a fish so big that it makes a whale look like a sardine.

ADDITIONAL POEMS

"About the Teeth of Sharks" by John Ciardi from *For Laughing Out Loud,* edited by Jack Prelutsky.

"Fish" by Mary Ann Hoberman from *Yellow Butter, Purple Jelly, Red Jam, Black Bread.*

"Melinda Mae" by Shel Silverstein from *Where the Sidewalk Ends.*

"Oh, Please Take Me Fishing" by Jack Prelutsky from *A Pizza the Size of the Sun.*

"The Water-Go-Round" by Dennis Lee from *The Ice Cream Store.*

"Why It's Hard to Be Romantic If You're an Octopus" by Jeff Moss from *The Other Side of the Door.*

ADDITIONAL SONGS AND
MUSICAL ACTIVITIES

"At the Codfish Ball" by The Chenille Sisters from *1-2-3 for Kids.*

"Billy the Squid" by Tom Chapin from *Billy the Squid.*

"Fish Are Orderly" by Tom Paxton from *I've Got a Yo-Yo.*

"Our Oceans" by Frank Cappelli from *Take a Seat.*

"Rubber Blubber Whale" by John McCutcheon from *Howjadoo.*

ADDITIONAL FINGERPLAYS AND
MOVEMENT ACTIVITIES

"I Hold My Fingers Like a Fish"
traditional

> I hold my fingers like a fish
> > *(Place palms together and wave them like fish moving)*
> And wave them as I go.
> See them swimming with a swish,
> So swiftly to and fro.

"The Sea Shell"
traditional

> I found a great big shell one day,
> > *(Cup hands)*
> It came from the ocean floor.
> I held it close up to my ear
> > *(Cupped hands by ear)*
> And heard the ocean roar.

VIDEOS

Burt Dow: Deep-Water Man. Weston Woods. (9 min.)

The Great White Man-Eating Shark. Weston Woods. (10 min.)

What'cha Gonna Wear?

Program at a Glance

MUSIC	"Jenny Jenkins" from the recording *Great Big Hits* by Sharon, Lois and Bram
PICTURE BOOK	*How Do I Put It On?* by Shigeo Watanabe
POEM	"Why Is It?" from *Falling Up* by Shel Silverstein
MUSICAL ACTIVITY	"What You Gonna Wear" from *Help Yourself* by Cathy Fink and Marcy Marxer
PICTURE BOOK	*Mrs. Toggle's Zipper* by Robin Pulver
PICTURE BOOK	*Froggy Gets Dressed* by Jonathan London
MUSICAL ACTIVITY	"This Is the Way We Dress Ourselves"
PICTURE BOOK	*Jesse Bear, What Will You Wear?* by Nancy White Carlstrom
FELT STORY	"My Kitten's Mittens" from *1-2-3 Colors: Colorful Activities for Young Children* by Jean Warren
MUSICAL ACTIVITY	"If Your Clothes Have Any Red" adapted by Rob Reid
PICTURE BOOK	*Animals Should Definitely Not Wear Clothing* by Judi Barrett

Preparation and Presentation

Invite the public to dress up in wild or fancy fashions. Dress yourself in a colorful array of clothing. Have a stuffed teddy bear on hand to help teach everyone how to dress the correct way. Play the song "Jenny Jenkins."

How Do I Put It On?
Shigeo Watanabe

Little Bear learns the hard way how to get dressed. In the end, he is proud that he got dressed "all by himself." Review the story for the audience with the help of the teddy bear and small articles of clothing. Put short pants on the teddy's head, and ask the audience if that is right. Put socks on the teddy bear's ears, and ask "How are we doing?" They'll straighten you out fast enough.

"Why Is It?"
Shel Silverstein

Show the audience Silverstein's drawing of a child with its clothes on wrong.

"What You Gonna Wear?"
Cathy Fink and Marcy Marxer

Sing this simple tune yourself or play the recording. The song asks "what you gonna wear" for various types of weather situations. The audience responds with an appropriate answer. Feel free to accept suggestions from the audience that vary from the examples found on the recording.

Mrs. Toggle's Zipper
Robin Pulver

All of the stories and songs so far have been about putting clothing *on*. Now read the Mrs. Toggle story about a teacher who has trouble getting her winter coat *off*. The book shows what could happen when the "thingamajig" on the zipper breaks off.

Froggy Gets Dressed
Jonathan London

This is one of my favorite read-alouds! The audience can help make several sound effects. Froggy hops out to play in the snow with a "zoop" of his socks, a "zup" of his boots, and a "zip" of his pants. Teach the parents to shout "FRRROGGYY" and the children to reply "Wha-a-a-t?"

"This Is the Way We Dress Ourselves"
traditional

Sing this to the tune of "Here We Go Round the Mulberry Bush." Inform the group that perhaps we should have taught Froggy this song so he wouldn't have forgotten how to get dressed. Have the audience stand and act out the motions.

1. This is the way we put on our pants,
   Put on our pants, put on our pants,
   This is the way we put on our pants
   So early in the morning.

2. This is the way we put on our shirt . . .

3. This is the way we pull up our socks . . .

Add verses for coats, scarves, boots, hats, and mittens. Vary clothing articles for the different seasons. Come up with unusual touches such as "This is the way we Velcro our sneakers."

Jesse Bear, What Will You Wear?
Nancy White Carlstrom

Carlstrom's book has a dance-like verse that's fun to read aloud. Jesse decides to wear his shirt of red, a rose between his toes, rice in his hair, and his p.j.s on his feet. You might want to dedicate a round of "This Is the Way We Dress Ourselves" to Jesse. "This is the way Jesse puts rice in his hair."

"My Kitten's Mittens"
Jean Warren

Make a felt kitten and felt mittens. Patterns and text can be found in Jean Warren's book *1-2-3 Colors* (or just create your own simple kitten and mitten patterns). Attach the felt mittens to the props mentioned in the verses and scatter them around the story area. Pluck the proper mitten off the props as you read each verse.

I usually adapt the verses to go along with features of the story area. "I found a mitten just right for a kitten on this clock so round. But, alas, the mitten was not the right mitten, for it was colored brown." I also match up pink with "a dinosaur's wink" (a dinosaur puppet), yellow with "a furry fellow" (another puppet), and red with "overhead" (a light fixture). I also tape the blue mittens to the bottom of my shoes and start "crying" because I can't find them. While I'm "crying," the bottoms of my shoes are exposed to the audience and they start shrieking "There they are!" If the kids don't pick up my not-so-subtle clues, the parents help by pointing.

"If Your Clothes Have Any Red"
traditional, adapted by Rob Reid

I have heard several different versions of "If Your Clothes Have Any Red" sung to the tune of "If You're Happy and You Know It." Some of the traditional verses include "if your clothes have any red, put your finger on your head" and "if your clothes have any blue, put your finger on your shoe." I added the following offbeat lyrics and motions:

> If your clothes have any yellow . . . turn your body into Jell-O . . .
> If your clothes have any brown . . . stand up and turn around . . .
> If your clothes have any blue . . . stick your nose inside your shoe . . .
> If your clothes have any purple . . . make the sound of a slurp-le . . .

If your clothes have any pink . . . give Rob a great big
  wink . . .
If your clothes have any white . . . give your neighbor a
  great big fright—BOO!

Animals Should Definitely Not Wear Clothing
Judi Barrett

Finish the program with this quick read. Ron Barrett's hilarious illustrations include a sheep wearing a wool sweater, a giraffe with several neckties, and a pair of pants on a hen who is trying to lay an egg.

Mix and Match

ADDITIONAL PICTURE BOOKS

Miller, Margaret. *Where Does It Go?*

> Where does a pair of socks belong? On a dog's paw? On a child's nose? No, on his feet. Children will giggle when they see the silly places the author suggests for various household objects.

Munsch, Robert. *Thomas' Snowsuit.*

> Whenever the grownups in Thomas's life want him to put on his new brown snowsuit, Thomas says "NNNNNO" and trouble erupts.

Sharratt, Nick. *My Mom and Dad Make Me Laugh.*

> Mom likes to wear spots, and Dad likes stripes. When they go to a safari park, Mom likes the leopards while Dad prefers the zebras. This is a good companion book to the song "Polka Dots, Checks and Stripes" sung by Parachute Express on their recording *Happy to Be Here.*

Small, David. *Fenwick's Suit.*

> This absurd tale will be appreciated by those parents who work in offices. Fenwick's suit goes off to work without him and no one even misses Fenwick.

ADDITIONAL POETRY

"Hand-Me-Downs" by Bob Zanger from *A Bad Case of the Giggles*, edited by Bruce Lansky.

"I Can Put My Socks On" by Tony Bradman from *Poems for the Very Young*, edited by Michael Rosen.

"Long Johns" by N. M. Bodecker from *Hurry, Hurry, Mary Dear and Other Nonsense Poems*.

"New Jacket" by Mary Ann Hoberman from *Fathers, Mothers, Sisters, Brothers: A Collection of Family Poems*.

"Stocking and Shirt" by James Reeves from *Once upon a Rhyme*, edited by Sara and Stephen Corrin.

ADDITIONAL SONGS AND MUSICAL ACTIVITIES

"The Dressing Song" by Michael Feinstein from *Pure Imagination*.

"I Can Put My Clothes On by Myself" by Hap Palmer from *Peek-a-Boo*.

"I Had an Old Coat" by Sharon, Lois and Bram from *Elephant Party*.

"Once I Saw Three Goats" by Sharon, Lois and Bram from *Singing 'n' Swinging*.

"Polka Dots, Checks and Stripes" by Parachute Express from *Happy to Be Here*.

"Underwear" by Barry Louis Polisar from *Teacher's Favorites*.

ADDITIONAL FINGERPLAYS AND MUSICAL ACTIVITIES

"I Can Tie My Own Shoes"
traditional

(Act out the motions)

> I can tie my shoelaces,
> I can brush my hair,

I can wash my face and hands
And dry myself with care.
I can clean my teeth, too,
Fasten up my frocks,
I can dress all by myself
And pull up both my socks.

"Miss Mary Mack"
traditional
This popular jumping-rope song can be done as a clapping chant.
Verse 1: Clap on "Mack," "black," "buttons," and "back."
Verse 2: Clap on "Mack," "purple," "buttons," and "girdle."

Miss Mary Mack, Mack, Mack,
All dressed in black, black, black,
With silver buttons, buttons, buttons,
All down her back, back, back.

Miss Mary Mack, Mack, Mack,
All dressed in purple, purple, purple,
With silver buttons, buttons, buttons,
All down her girdle, girdle, girdle.

ADDITIONAL FELT ACTIVITY

"A Little Girl Named Riding Hood"
Rob Reid

This activity was inspired by Jean Warren's "My Kitten's Mittens." Make a felt cutout of a little girl and hooded-cloak garments of colors mentioned in the text. Patterns can be fashioned from illustrations found in the various editions of Little Red Riding Hood.

A little girl named Riding Hood
Found a hood of green.
"This little hood, why, it's no good,
Reminds me of a bean,

Marine, Martian queen,
Reminds me of a bean."

A little girl named Riding Hood
Found a hood of white.
"This little hood, why, it's no good,
Reminds me of frostbite,
Termite, pillow fight,
Reminds me of frostbite."

A little girl named Riding Hood
Found a hood of pink.
"This little hood, why, it's no good,
That color sure does stink,
Hot wink, lemon drink,
That color sure does stink."

A little girl named Riding Hood
Found a hood of blue.
"This little hood, why, it's no good,
It makes me think of you,
How true, Gran's hairdo,
It makes me think of you."

A little girl named Riding Hood
Found a hood of red.
"This little hood, it's really good,
I'm off to Granny's bed,
Well-read wolf ahead,
I'm off to Granny's bed."

VIDEOS

Charlie Needs a Cloak. Weston Woods. (8 min.)
The Flyaway Pantaloons. Living Oak Media. (6 min.)
The Purple Coat. Reading Rainbow.

What's Cooking?

$\overline{\qquad}$ *Program at a Glance* $\overline{\qquad}$

MUSIC — "Corner Grocery Store" from *Corner Grocery Store* by Raffi

POEM — "I Love You, I Love You"

PICTURE BOOK — *The Wolf's Chicken Stew* by Kaiko Kasza

MUSICAL ACTIVITY — "Apples and Bananas/Lima Beans and Diced Beets" adapted by Rob Reid

PICTURE BOOK — *I Know an Old Lady Who Swallowed a Pie* by Alison Jackson

POEM — "Lunch Box" from *You Be Good and I'll Be Night* by Eve Merriam

STORY — "The Super-Duper Peanut Butter and Jelly Sandwich" adapted by Rob Reid

PICTURE BOOK — *Lunch* by Denise Fleming

PICTURE BOOK — *The Very Hungry Caterpillar* by Eric Carle

FINGERPLAY — "Two Fat Sausages"

PICTURE BOOK — *Hunky Dory Ate It* by Katie Evans

MUSICAL ACTIVITY — "Jelly, Jelly, in My Belly" from *The Elephant Show Record* by Sharon, Lois and Bram

Preparation and Presentation

Don an apron and a chef's hat. Set a variety of cooking utensils on a table. Sprinkle the table liberally with books. Play Raffi's "Corner Grocery Store" as the audience enters the story area. You're ready for a library cooking show.

"I Love You, I Love You"
anonymous

This silly, short poem always gets a laugh. It sets the tone for the rest of the program.

> I love you, I love you,
> I love you divine.
> Please give me your bubblegum,
> You're sitting on mine.

The Wolf's Chicken Stew
Keiko Kasza

A wolf tries to fatten up a chicken by dropping off pancakes, doughnuts, and a cake for her. When her chicks give the wolf one hundred kisses, I ask the audience to simulate that many kisses.

"Apples and Bananas/Lima Beans and Diced Beets"
traditional, adapted by Rob Reid

Many school age children know the vowel-tricky song "Apples and Bananas." The phrase "I like to eat, eat, eat apples and bananas" is sung over and over with each repetition emphasizing each of the long vowel sounds (a, e, i, o, u). Thus, the phrases sound like "I like to ate, ate, ate, ay-ples and bay-nay-nays," and "I like to eat, eat, eat, ee-ples and bee-nee-nees," and so forth. The presence of teens and adults makes this exercise flow smoothly with lots of laughs. Some musicians apply the same technique to other phrases, such as "pepperoni pizza." Here's my treatment called "Lima Beans and Diced Beets."

> I like to eat, eat, eat, lima beans and diced beets . . .
> *(repeat each phrase)*
> I like to ate, ate, ate, lay-may baynes and dayced baytes . . .
> I like to eat, eat, eat, lee-mee beans and deeced beets . . .
> I like to ite, ite, ite, lie-my bines and diced bites . . .
> I like to oat, oat, oat, low-mow bones and doced boats . . .
> I like to ute, ute, ute, lu-mu bunes and duced boots . . .

Musician Hans Mayer likes to "read, read, read books and magazines" on his recording *See Ya Later, Alligator*. Try the vowel treatment on that phrase.

The original words and tune of "Apples and Bananas" can be found on several recordings including Raffi's *One Light, One Sun* and Nancy Cassidy's *Kids' Songs*.

I Know an Old Lady Who Swallowed a Pie
Alison Jackson

This hilarious take-off of "I Know an Old Lady Who Swallowed a Fly" shows an old lady who swallows a salad ("she was looking quite pallid"), a turkey ("her future looked murky"), and more until she becomes the size of a parade balloon. This Thanksgiving book can be read with great success throughout the year.

"Lunch Box"
Eve Merriam

This is a good prop poem. Attach the words of the poem inside the lid of a kid's lunch box and pantomine eating the food while you recite.

"The Super-Duper Peanut Butter and Jelly Sandwich"
traditional, adapted by Rob Reid

Here is a variation of a story we used to tell as kids. As you recite the part about peanut butter getting stuck to the roof of your mouth, talk with your tongue actually on the roof of your mouth. Draw out the words "roof" and "spoon." The sound is hilarious. Embellish the story to make it your own.

I like to make what I call a Super-Duper-Peanut-Butter-and-Jelly Sandwich. All you do is take one slice of bread *(pantomime building the sandwich and all following actions)*, about two or three inches of peanut butter—chunky style, of course—and then put some jelly on top of that. Aw heck, put the whole jar of jelly on it. Put another slice of bread on top of that and take a big bite.

Trouble is . . . *(start talking as if the peanut butter is stuck to the top of your mouth)* the peanut butter gets stuck to the roooof of your mouth. And you can't very well tell stories with peanut butter stuck to the roooof of your mouth.

I have found the best way to get peanut butter off the roooof of your mouth is to take a spoooon. Stick the spoooon inside your mouth and remove all the peanut butter off the roooof of your mouth *(talk normally)* . . . like this.

But now you have peanut butter on your spoon. What if you wanted to use that spoon for soup or cereal? Take your finger and run it alongside the inside of your spoon so that all of the peanut butter is off the spoon . . . and onto your finger.

Oh no. What if you want to use your finger to use the elevator or type on the computer? Lick all the peanut butter off your finger and . . . *(talk in the funny voice again)* now it's back on the roooof of your mouth. But that's okay because it tastes just as good the second time around. But you know and I know that the BEST way to get peanut butter off the rooof of your mouth is with a spoooon. *(Normal voice)* Right?"

Lunch
Denise Fleming

The Very Hungry Caterpillar
Eric Carle

Both books are about tiny critters who eat colorful food.

"Two Fat Sausages"
traditional

Instruct the audience to practice making a popping sound in their mouths with their finger or thumb. They'll need to be able to do it for this fingerplay. I tell the kids that they can practice the popping noise right after storytime, they can practice during the ride home, they can practice during meal-time, they can practice right before bed . . . and then I catch the eyes of the parents and say, "Umm, perhaps you better just practice outside once in awhile. . . ."

> Two fat sausages
> > *(Hold up both thumbs)*
> Sizzling in the pan
> > *(Move thumbs)*
> One went POP!
> > *(Make the popping noise)*
> And one went BLAM!
> > *(Clap on "BLAM")*

Hunky Dory Ate It
Katie Evans

This is a very short rhyming book about a dog who eats too much food. The audience can chime "Hunky Dory ate it" throughout the story.

"Jelly, Jelly, in My Belly"
traditional

Chant "2-4-6-8. Tell me what is on your plate." Then chant or sing the following verses. (The melody can be heard on the recording *The Elephant Show Record* by Sharon, Lois and Bram.)

> We're going to have some jelly.
> Hurray! Hurray!
> We're going to have some jelly.
> Hurray! Hurray!

Jelly for our dinner,
Jelly every day,
Jelly, jelly, in our belly.
Hip, hip, hip, hooray!

Instruct the audience to raise their fists for "Hip, hip, hip, hooray!" Then ask them to name another type of food. Repeat the game with their suggestion.

We're going to have some pizza.
Hurray! Hurray!
We're going to have some pizza.
Hurray! Hurray!
Pizza for our dinner,
Pizza every day,
And jelly, jelly, in our belly.
Hip, hip, hip, hooray!

Keep adding suggestions. Before the last line of the song, everyone has to recite all previous foods mentioned. Since my memory is faulty, I sometimes draw crude renditions of the foods mentioned on a drawing pad and refer back to it. Others like the challenge of memorizing the list. Here's how the song would sound at the end if "apples," "candy," and "macaroni and cheese" were added throughout the game:

We're going to have macaroni and cheese.
Hurray! Hurray!
We're going to have macaroni and cheese.
Hurray! Hurray!
Macaroni and cheese for dinner,
Macaroni and cheese every day,
(*Spoken*) And candy and apples and pizza and . . .
(*Sing*) Jelly, jelly, in our belly.
Hip, hip, hip, hooray!

Mix and Match

ADDITIONAL PICTURE BOOKS

Brown, Marc. *D. W. the Picky Eater.*

> D. W. refuses to eat the food set before her—until she tries a piece of Little Bo Peep Pot Pie.

Chapman, Cheryl. *Pass the Fritters, Critters.*

> Several animals refuse to pass food to a child until the child uses the magic word "please." Fun rhymes include "pass the cobbler, Gobbler" and "thanks for the cider, spider."

Hayes, Sarah. *Eat Up, Gemma.*

> Baby Gemma is a picky eater until she tries to eat the fake fruit on a woman's hat.

Priceman, Marjorie. *How to Make an Apple Pie and See the World.*

> Apple pies can be difficult to make if you need to travel all over the world to obtain the ingredients. This is a good story to tell with a globe on hand.

Sharmat, Mitchell. *Gregory, the Terrible Eater.*

> Gregory is a goat who refuses to eat the normal goat fare, such as shoes and tin cans.
>
> I once had a puppeteer make a goat puppet that could "swallow" small objects. The children would then "feed" it small objects once storytime was done.

Torres, Leyla. *Saturday Sancocho.*

> Maria Lili and Mama Ana go to the market square where they cleverly barter for the ingredients to make chicken sancocho.

ADDITIONAL POEMS

"If You're No Good at Cooking" by Kit Wright from *Poems for the Very Young,* edited by Michael Rosen.

"Rattlesnake Meat" by Ogden Nash from *For Laughing Out Loud,* edited by Jack Prelutsky.

"Stomache Suprise" by Geraldine Nicholas from *Kids Pick the Funniest Poems,* edited by Bruce Lansky.

"Two Sad" by William Cole from *Read-Aloud Rhymes for the Very Young,* edited by Jack Prelutsky.

"When Tillie Ate the Chili" by Jack Prelutsky from *The New Kid on the Block.*

"Yellow Butter" by Mary Ann Hoberman from *Yellow Butter, Purple Jelly, Red Jam, Black Bread.*

ADDITIONAL SONGS AND MUSICAL ACTIVITIES

"Biscuits in the Oven" by Raffi from *Baby Beluga.*

"I Am a Pizza" by Charlotte Diamond from *10 Carrot Diamond.*

"Meatballs and Spaghetti" by Bonnie Phipps from *Dinosaur Choir.*

"Stone Soup" by Tom Chapin from *Mother Earth.*

"Watermelon" by John McCutcheon from *Family Garden.*

ADDITIONAL FINGERPLAYS AND MOVEMENT ACTIVITIES

"Five Plump Peas"
traditional

> Five plump peas
> > *(Make a fist with thumb tucked in)*
> in a pea pod pressed,
> One grew,
> > *(Hold up one finger)*
> Two grew,
> > *(Hold up two fingers)*
> and so did all the rest.
> > *(Hold up five fingers)*
> They grew . . .
> > *(Hands in front, palms together)*

and they grew . . .
>   *(Pull hands apart)*

and they grew . . .
>   *(Hands farther apart)*

and never stopped.
>   *(Hands wide apart)*

They grew so fat that the pea pod
Popped!
>   *(Clap hands)*

"The Pancake"
traditional

Mix a pancake, stir a pancake,
>   *(Make stirring motions)*

Pop it in the pan.
>   *(Make pouring motion)*

Fry the pancake,
>   *(Move imaginary frying pan)*

Toss the pancake,
>   *(Toss it in the air)*

Catch it if you can.
>   *(Catch the pancake with the pan)*

VIDEOS

Cloudy with a Chance of Meatballs. Living Oak Media. (12 min.)

Frog Goes to Dinner. Phoenix Films. (12 min.)

Wild Critters

Program at a Glance

MUSIC	"A Place in the Choir" from *Hug the Earth* by Tickle Tune Typhoon
POEM	"Always Be Kind to Animals" by John Gardner
PICTURE BOOK	*Bearsie Bear and the Surprise Sleepover Party* by Bernard Waber
MOVEMENT ACTIVITY	"Animal Sounds in Different Languages"
MOVEMENT ACTIVITY	"Can You Growl Like a Tiger?"
PICTURE BOOK	*The Great Ball Game* by Joseph Bruchac
PICTURE BOOK	*Wombat Stew* by Marcia Vaughn
POEM	"Two Skunks"
FINGERPLAY	"Three Little Smelly Skunks" by Rob Reid
PICTURE BOOK	*Peck Slither and Slide* by Suse MacDonald

Preparation and Presentation

Ask audience members to bring their favorite stuffed giraffes, wolves, zebras, lions, and other wild critters. Decorate the room with animal puppets and plants. Create patterns of different animal tracks from reference books, draw and cut them out of black construction paper, and tack them to the walls. Let audience members guess whose tracks they are.

Play the song "A Place in the Choir." The song is also known as "All God's Critters" and can be found on the recordings *Down the Do-Re-Mi* by Red Grammer, *Howjadoo* by John McCutcheon, and *The Happy Wanderer* by Bill Staines, the composer of the song.

"Always Be Kind to Animals"
John Gardner

This short poem will elicit a laugh as you warn your listeners about an animal's bite.

Bearsie Bear and the Surprise Sleepover Party
Bernard Waber

This hilarious book features Bearsie Bear who lets Moosie Moose, Cowsie Cow, Piggie Pig, Foxie Fox, Goosie Goose, and Porkie Porcupine into his cabin. The dialogue is great to read aloud. " 'It's me, Piggie Pig,' said Piggie Pig. 'Piggie Pig?' said Cowsie Cow. 'Piggie Pig?' said Moosie Moose. 'Piggie Pig?' said Bearsie Bear? 'Yes, Piggie Pig,' said Piggie Pig." Great potential for reader's theater.

"Animal Sounds in Different Languages"
Tell the audience that the words for animal sounds are different in the various cultures. Ask them to make the sound of a monkey and act like one. Inform them that a monkey sounds like "Keek-keek" in Japanese. A monkey also sounds like "Twee-twee" in Swedish and "Szeek-szeek" in Polish. Share the following animal sounds:

Birds: Pechiko-pachiko (Japan)
Czwir-czwir (Poland)
Ji-ji (China)
Trit-trit (Indonesia)

Frog: Kroo-kroo (Swahili)
Gedo Gedo (Japan)
Kwok Kwok (Germany)

Bees: Hmmm! Hmmm! (India)
Weng-weng (Japan)
Sorr-orr (Sweden)

Dogs: Huf-huf (Hebrew)
Hong-hong (Thailand)
Mong-mong (Korea)

"Can You Growl Like a Tiger?"
traditional, adapted by Rob Reid

Have the audience stand and stretch for this activity.

> Can you growl like a tiger?
> Can you hop like a frog?
> Can you climb like a monkey?
> Can you bark like a dog?
>
> Can you slither like a snake?
> Can you fly like a bat?
> Can you howl like a wolf?
> Can you stre-ttttt-cccchhh like a cat?

If the adults are reluctant to act out these motions, pit them against the kids with a comment like, "Let's do it again and see who can do a better job—the adults or the kids."

The Great Ball Game
Joseph Bruchac

This Muskogee story describes how the bat was chosen to be an animal instead of a bird.

Wombat Stew
Marcia Vaughn

Clever Dingo catches Wombat and plans to make a stew. Platypus, Emu, Lizard, Echidna, and Koala devise a plan to rescue Wombat. The audience can dance the Dingo dance and sing the chorus "Wombat stew, wombat stew / Gooey, brewy / Yummy, chewy / Wombat stew."

"Two Skunks"
anonymous

> There were two skunks—
> Out and In.
> When In was out,
> Out was in.
> One day Out was in and In was out.
> Their mother,
> who was in with Out,
> wanted In in.
> "Bring In in,"
> she said to Out.
> So Out went out
> and brought In in.
> How did you find him
> so fast?" she asked.
> "Instinct," he said.

"Three Little Smelly Skunks"
Rob Reid

Have the audience hold up three fingers on "three." On "little," have them indicate little with their thumb and pointer finger. On "smelly," have them hold their noses.

> Three little smelly skunks,
> Sleeping on their smelly bunks,
>> *(Lay head on hands)*
> Didn't hear an owl sneak in.
>> *(Point to ear, shake head, flap arms)*

"Whoo-whoo" woke them
Quick as a wink.
    (Look surprised)
One forgot to spray its stink.
    (Hold nose)
Now there are two smelly skunks.
    (Hold up two fingers)

Two little smelly skunks,
    (Repeat motions)
Sleeping in their smelly bunks,
Didn't hear a man sneak in.
"Gotcha!" woke them
Quick as a wink.
One forgot to spray its stink.
Now there is one smelly skunk.

One little smelly skunk,
Sleeping on its smelly bunk,
Didn't hear a dog sneak in.
"Woof-woof" woke it
Quick as a wink.
It REMEMBERED to spray its stink.
Now there is one smelly dog.
    (Howl like a dog)

Peck Slither and Slide
Suse MacDonald

MacDonald demonstrates how various animals move and interact. Penguins slide, apes swing, giraffes reach, beavers build, and woodpeckers peck. The audience can act out the motions as you read.

Mix and Match

ADDITIONAL PICTURE BOOKS

Andrae, Giles. *Rumble in the Jungle.*

Here is a colorful, poetic look at hippos, leopards, lions, and other not-so-fearsome jungle and plains animals. Look for the flea-munching chimps and the zebra who thinks his stripes are cool.

Hadithi, Mwenye. *Lazy Lion*.

Lion orders the other animals to build him a house. The white ants can only build a house of earth, the weaver-birds only build nests of grass, the aardvarks only build tunnels and caves, and the crocodiles just make wet, river-bank caves. That is why Lion sleeps on the open plain.

Harley, Bill. *Sitting Down to Eat*.

Elephant, tiger, bear, lion, hippo, rhino, crocodile, and whale all crowd in a tiny house. When caterpillar joins them, the house goes BOOM. A musical variation of this story can be found on Harley's recording *Come on Out and Play*.

Rogers, Sally. *Earthsong*.

This picture book is based on the song "Over in the Endangered Meadow" by Sally Rogers, who created this ecological version of the folksong "Over in the Meadow." While sharing the book, play her song from the recording *Piggyback Planet*.

Wolf, Jake. *What You Do Is Easy, What I Do Is Hard*.

A squirrel argues with a bee, an ant, a spider, and a robin about who has the hardest life. The squirrel sets out to prove he can build a web, collect some pollen, dig for earthworms, and gather crumbs.

ADDITIONAL POEMS

"The Bat" by Doug Florian from *Beast Feast*.

"Giraffes" by Mary Ann Hoberman from *Eric Carle's Animals Animals*, edited by Eric Carle.

"Lion" by N. M. Bodecker from *More Surprises*, edited by Lee Bennett Hopkins.

"The Panther" by Ogden Nash from *Custard and Company.*

"Tiger" by Mary Ann Hoberman from Y*ellow Butter, Purple Jelly, Red Jam, Black Bread.*

"Tom Tigercat" by J. Patrick Lewis from *For Laughing Out Louder,* edited by Jack Prelutsky.

ADDITIONAL SONGS AND MUSICAL ACTIVITIES

"Animal Tales" by Bill Shontz from *Animal Tales.*

"Deep in the Jungle" by Joe Scruggs from *Deep in the Jungle.*

"Gned the Gnu" by Gary Rosen from *Tot Rock.*

"Everybody's Got to Have a Home" by Bill Shontz from *Animal Tales.*

"Goin' to the Zoo" by Tom Paxton from *Goin' to the Zoo.*

ADDITIONAL FINGERPLAYS AND MOVEMENT ACTIVITIES

"Five Little Monkeys"
traditional

> Five little monkeys
> > *(Hold up five fingers)*
> Swinging from a tree.
> > *(Move fingers back and forth)*
> Teasing Alligator
> "Can't catch me!"
> > *(Thumbs in ears, wiggle fingers)*
>
> Along came Alligator
> > *(Make a mouth with other hand)*
> Slowly as can be,
> Then SNAP!
> > *(Grab one finger with the "mouth" hand)*
>
> Four little monkeys . . .
>
> > *(Repeat down to no little monkeys)*

"Squirrel's Got a Bushy Tail"
traditional, adapted by Rob Reid

> Squirrel's got a bushy tail,
> Shake that tail,
> > *(Shake hips)*
> Shake that tail.
> Squirrel's got a bushy tail,
> Shake that tail now!
>
> Elephant's got a curly trunk,
> Move that trunk,
> > *(Arm in front of nose, move arm)*
> Move that trunk.
> Elephant's got a curly trunk,
> Move that trunk now!
>
> Raccoon's got a dark, black mask,
> Show that mask,
> > *(Form a diamond shape with the pointer and middle
> > fingers of both hands by joining them over eyes)*
> Show that mask,
> Raccoon's got a dark, black mask,
> Show that mask now!
>
> Gator's got a great big jaw,
> Snap that jaw,
> > *(Make a jaw with both arms and hands, clap)*
> Snap that jaw.
> Gator's got a great big jaw,
> Snap that jaw now!

Make up your own verses with the help of the audience.

VIDEOS

Over in the Meadow. Weston Woods. (9 min.)

Why Mosquitoes Buzz in People's Ears. Weston Woods.
(10 min.)

Winter Wonderland

Program at a Glance

MUSIC	*Wintersongs* by John McCutcheon
PICTURE BOOK	*The Hat* by Jan Brett
PICTURE BOOK	*Snip, Snip . . . Snow!* by Nancy Poydar
POEM	"Read This with Gestures" by John Ciardi from *Snowy Day: Stories and Poems* by Caroline Feller Bauer
PICTURE BOOK	*The Mitten* by Jan Brett
MUSIC	"The Mitten" from *Peanut Butter and Jelly's Greatest Hits* by Peanut Butter and Jelly
FINGERPLAY	"Three Little Snowmen" by Elizabeth Vollrath
PICTURE BOOK	*Midnight Snowman* by Caroline Feller Bauer
FINGERPLAY	"I Am a Snowman"
PICTURE BOOK	*Snowballs* by Lois Ehlert
CRAFT	Make a Snow Family

Preparation and Presentation

Bring several small items from home for the craft activity. Ask the audience to bring items, also. These include buttons, tiny toys, bells, office supplies, hardware, cloth scraps, yarn, dry foods, old keys—anything. These items will be used to build snowmen, snow women, and snow creatures based on Lois Ehlert's book *Snowballs*.

Decorate the story area with paper snowflakes hanging from the ceiling. Have volunteers help make them.

Play any song from John McCutcheon's recording *Wintersongs* as the audience enters the story area. My favorites on the recording include "Soup," "Hot Chocolate," "Hibernation," and "Tommy, Don't Lick That Pipe."

Greet the audience wearing a winter hat, scarf, boots, and gloves. Make sure they can be easily removed after the first story lest you get too hot in them.

The Hat
Jan Brett

A hedgehog winds up with a woolen winter stocking stuck on his head. He tells the other animals that it is his winter hat. They all laugh at him but soon find themselves wanting winter clothing to wear on their heads.

Snip, Snip . . . Snow!
Nancy Poydar

Sophie is tired of waiting for it to snow. She convinces her teacher to have the class make paper snowflakes. Just as soon as they finish, the real snow starts to fall.

"Read This with Gestures"
John Ciardi

Ask everyone to stand and act out this poem about the proper way to throw a snowball.

The Mitten
Jan Brett

This companion volume to Brett's *The Hat* is based on the popular folk tale in which several animals crawl into a mitten to escape the cold. This is a good story for audience members to act out. Grab a large sheet to represent the mitten. Have children act out the parts of the smaller animals, teens act out the parts of the owl and badger, and adults play the fox and bear. Ask a brave toddler (with perhaps the help of mom or dad) to play the role of the tiny mouse who "bursts" the mitten apart (toss the sheet in the air).

"The Mitten"
Peanut Butter and Jelly

The song is based on the folk tale of the same name. Play the recording and have the audience join in on the catchy chorus:

> Who's gonna make this mitten their home,
> Skittle do, skittle day, dilly dally oh shay.

"Three Little Snowmen"
Elizabeth Vollrath

> One little, two little, three little snowmen
> *(Hold up three fingers, one at a time)*
> Playing in the sun,
> *(Dance fingers around)*
> One little, two little, three little snowmen
> Having lots of fun.
>
> One little, two little, three little snowmen
> *(Hold up three fingers, one at a time)*
> Sliding on the ice,
> *(Slide fingers around)*
> One little, two little, three little snowmen
> Said, "This is nice!"

One little, two little, three little snowmen
 (Hold up three fingers, one at a time)
Looked at the sun up high,
 (Stretch fingers upward)
One little, two little, three little snowmen
Each gave a great big sigh.

One little, two little, three little snowmen
 (Hold up three fingers, one at a time)
Began to melt away,
 (Slowly bend fingers, down into fist)
One little, two little, three little snowmen
Said, "We'll be back some winter day!"

Midnight Snowman
Caroline Feller Bauer

This story will be a hit in those regions that usually don't receive snow. Snow is such a novelty to the characters that when it does snow, the whole neighborhood builds a colossal snowman.

"I Am a Snowman"
traditional

Have everyone stand. Yes, even the big folks!

I am a snowman, cold and white,
 (Point to self)
I stand so tall through all the night,
 (Stretch tall)
With a carrot nose
 (Point to nose)
And a head held high
 (Point to head)
And a lump of coal for each eye.
 (Point to eyes)
I have a scarf all made of red
 (Point to neck)

And a hat upon my head.
   (Point to top of head)
Look! The sun is out! Oh my!
   (Point overhead)
I think that I am going to cry!
   (Pretend to cry)
Yesterday I was plump and round,
   (Form circle around middle with arms)
Now, I'm just a puddle on the ground.
   (Slowly sink to floor)

Snowballs
Lois Ehlert

Ehlert decorates a snow dad, a snow mom, a snow boy, a snow girl, a snow baby, a snow cat, and a snow dog with buttons, leaves, seeds, yarn, and other natural and household materials.

Make a Snow Family
based on Lois Ehlert's *Snowballs*

Make several snowmen cutouts before the program. Have volunteers help cut out several sizes. Spread on a table the tiny materials the audience brought. Supply glue and scissors. Let the families decorate their own snow families and creatures in styles inspired by Ehlert's snow creations. Hang them on the library walls throughout the winter before returning them to the families.

Mix and Match

ADDITIONAL PICTURE BOOKS

Christiansen, Candace. *The Mitten Tree.*

> An elderly woman notices children without mittens at the bus stop. She knits mittens for them and hangs them on a tree outside her house in this heartfelt story.

Evans, Lezlie. *Snow Dance.*

Several children perform an improvised "whirling, swirling, twirling, begging flakes to come" dance to make the snow fall. Have your audience stand up and perform your own snow dance. (Pray the snow waits until after storytime!)

Gliori, Debi. *The Snowchild.*

The other children won't play with Katie, but when she builds a snowchild, she makes a new friend.

Keown, Elizabeth. *Emily's Snowball: The World's Biggest.*

Emily's snowball gets bigger and bigger—even bigger than a truck. It doesn't stop there. The neighbors get together and help Emily build a snow mountain.

Nielson, Laura F. *Jeremy's Muffler.*

Aunt Alice makes Jeremy a muffler that is so long that it gets caught in the school bus door and is used by fifth-graders as a jump rope. One fateful day, the extra-long muffler is used to save a child during an emergency.

ADDITIONAL POETRY

"Hurry, Hurry, Mary Dear" by N. M. Bodecker from *Hurry, Hurry, Mary Dear.*

"The Mitten Song" by Marie Louise Allen from *A New Treasury of Children's Poetry,* edited by Joanna Cole.

"The More It Snows" by A. A. Milne from *The House at Pooh Corner.*

"Skiing" by Marchette Chute from *Winter Poems,* edited by Barbara Rogasky.

"Snowballs" by Shel Silverstein from *Falling Up.*

"Winter Clothes" by Karla Kuskin from *The Random House Book of Poetry for Children,* edited by Jack Prelutsky.

ADDITIONAL SONGS AND
MUSICAL ACTIVITIES

"I Like to Be Cold and Wet" by Troubadour from *On the Trail.*

"Let's Play in the Snow" by Rachel Buchman from *Sing a Song of Seasons.*

"The Mitten" by Rachel Buchman from *Sing a Song of Seasons.*

"Snow Song" by Mary Lu Walker from *The Frog's Party.*

"So Cold Outside" by Fran Avni from *Artichokes and Brussel Sprouts.*

ADDITIONAL FINGERPLAYS AND
MOVEMENT ACTIVITIES

"Five Little Snowmen"
traditional

> Five little snowmen
> > *(Hold up five fingers)*
> Knocking at my door,
> > *("Knock" with other hand)*
> One melted away
> And then there were four.
> > *(Hold up four fingers)*
>
> Four little snowmen
> Playing with me,
> > *(Point to self)*
> One melted away
> And then there were three.
> > *(Hold up three fingers)*
>
> Three little snowmen
> Playing with you,
> > *(Point to "you")*
> One melted away
> And then there were two.
> > *(Hold up two fingers)*

Two little snowmen
Playing in the sun,
   (Point overhead)
One melted away
And then there was one.
   (Hold up one finger)

One little snowman
When the day was done,
Melted away
And then there were none.
   (Hold out empty hands)

"Here's a Great Big Hill"
traditional

Here's a great big hill
   (Point to self)
With snow all down the side.
   (Run hands up and down your sides)
Let's take our speedy sled
   (Hold out hand)
And down the hill we'll slide.
   (Run hand down side of body)

VIDEOS

Brave Irene. Weston Woods. (13 min.)

The Snowy Day. Weston Woods. (6 min.)

Woof & Wag

Program at a Glance

MUSIC	"My Dog's Bigger Than Your Dog" from *Goin' to the Zoo* by Tom Paxton
POEM	"I've Got a Dog"
PICTURE BOOK	*Three Stories You Can Read to Your Dog* by Sara Swan Miller
FINGERPLAY	"The Puppy and the Cat"
MUSICAL ACTIVITY	"Do Your Ears Hang Low?" from *Stay Tuned* by Sharon, Lois and Bram
CHAPTER BOOK	Selection from *Puppies, Dogs, and Blue Northers: Reflections on Being Raised by a Pack of Sled Dogs* by Gary Paulsen
MUSICAL ACTIVITY	"B-I-N-G-O" from *We All Live Together, Vol. 4,* by Greg and Steve
PICTURE BOOK	*Martha Speaks* by Susan Meddaugh
PICTURE BOOK	*Ten Dogs in the Window* by Claire Masurel
MUSICAL ACTIVITY	"How Much Is That Doggie in the Window?" from *Stay Tuned* by Sharon, Lois and Bram

Preparation and Presentation

As the audience enters, play the recording "My Dog's Bigger Than Your Dog" (a second-generation favorite). As with the "Meow and Squeak" theme, have the audience practice barking, woofing, whining, and howling to show their appreciation for each story and activity.

"I've Got a Dog"
anonymous

> I've got a dog as thin as a rail,
> He's got fleas all over his tail,
> Every time his tail goes flop,
> The fleas on the bottom all hop to the top.

If you have a dog puppet, scratch it all over while you read this poem. If you don't have a puppet, you can turn this into a fingerplay. Crook two fingers for the fleas and hop them around your body as if you were the dog.

Three Stories You Can Read to Your Dog
Sara Swan Miller

These three short stories are read as if directly to a dog. The adults will catch the subtle humor before the children. In one story, the dog hears "THUMPING." He assumes it is a burglar at the door and starts barking. Pretty soon, his owner comes "THUMPING" into the room and opens the door to show the dog that no one is there. Instead of being embarrassed, the dog is proud that his barking scared away the "burglar."

"The Puppy and the Cat"
traditional

> See my little puppy dog,
> *(Hold up one fist)*

See my little cat.
> *(Hold up other fist)*

Puppy goes to sleep
Just like that.
> *(Put head on hands)*

Kitty sneaks up quietly,
> *(Bring the "cat" fist near the other)*

Tickles puppy's chin.
> *(Tickle the "dog" fist with one finger)*

Puppy wakes up startled,
> *("Dog" fist wide open, fingers outstretched)*

Let the chase begin!
> *("Dog" fist chases "cat" fist in the air)*

"Do Your Ears Hang Low?"
traditional, adapted by Sharon, Lois and Bram

Do your ears hang low? Do they wobble to and fro?
Can you tie them in a knot? Can you tie them in a bow?
Can you throw them over your shoulder like a
> Continental soldier?

Do your ears hang low?

I'm afraid I'm going to be remembered in life as that guy who put tights on his head for "Do Your Ears Hang Low?" I used to sing this song with a floppy-eared dog puppet. One day, one of the moms came up after a program and told me that the dog ears reminded her of her childhood when all the neighbor kids ran around with tights on their heads. POP! The lightbulb went off over my head, and I've been putting tights on my head ever since. Try it and gauge your audience's reaction! Move the legs of the tights to the lyrics. Then follow up with Sharon, Lois and Bram's additional verses about twisting your nose, touching it with your tongue, pursing your lips and making them do the twist, blowing kisses and giving a crooked smile, wiggling your tongue, rolling your eyes, and closing with a "little wink—blink, blink, blink."

Selection from *Puppies, Dogs, and Blue Northers: Reflections on Being Raised by a Pack of Sled Dogs*
Gary Paulsen

Read the chapter titled "The Home Wreckers" from this wonderful recounting of life in northern Minnesota. Paulsen describes the calamity that occurs when he mischievously allows thirty puppies into his house while his wife and son are still asleep in bed. I rarely read passages from chapter books to mixed-aged groups, but Paulsen has the skill to enchant the very young as well as the adults.

"B-I-N-G-O"
traditional

> There was a farmer had a dog
> and Bingo was his name-o.
> B-I-N-G-O, B-I-N-G-O, B-I-N-G-O,
> and Bingo was his name-o.

Make five posterboard squares or felt circles and place one letter from the name Bingo on each. Have volunteers of all ages stand in a line holding the squares or circles. Each time you sing the song, have a volunteer flip the square or circle so the letter is no longer visible. Instruct the audience to clap when they see the blank shape. "(Clap)-I-N-G-O . . ." and so on. The visuals help the younger children understand the concept. One alternative to clapping is to bark. "(Bark)-(bark)-(bark)-G-O . . ." If you are not familiar with this popular tune, check out the recordings *We All Live Together, Vol. 4,* by Greg and Steve or *Sing A to Z* by Sharon, Lois and Bram. And by the way, is Bingo the farmer or the dog?

Martha Speaks
Susan Meddaugh

What would happen if a dog ate a bowl of alphabet soup and the letters traveled to her brain instead of her stomach? She'd be able to speak, of course. Martha, the dog, speaks up a storm. Invite a couple of adults and older children to read the book's dialogue balloons while you read the main text.

Ten Dogs in the Window
Claire Masurel

This backward-counting book shows ten dogs in the window of a pet store. The dogs are matched with owners one by one. This is a great lead-in for the following song.

"How Much Is That Doggie in the Window?"
adapted by Sharon, Lois and Bram

Divide the audience into three groups. Teach the first group to chant "Bull! Dog!" on the beat. Teach the second group to say "Chihuahua" and the third group to chant "Terrier," all the time keeping a steady beat. Add them all together and sing "How Much Is That Doggie in the Window?" over their chanting voices. This is one of the most enjoyable mixed-age activities I have done (and you definitely wouldn't be able to do it with the children alone). I highly recommend listening to the Sharon, Lois and Bram recording to fully understand the concept. They also sing it on the recording *Great Big Hits*.

Mix and Match

ADDITIONAL PICTURE BOOKS

Barracca, Debra, and Sal Barracca. *The Adventures of Taxi Dog*.

Maxi is a dog that rides around New York City all day with his owner, taxi driver Jim. Together they meet an opera singer, a troupe of clowns, and a lady in labor.

Ernst, Lisa Campbell. *Walter's Tail*.

Mrs. Tully's dog, Walter, has a tail that constantly wags. This tail knocks over jigsaw puzzle pieces, dainties from a clothesline, a barrel of lemon drops in a candy store, and a bottle of Pansy Perfume in a beauty shop. Walter's tail also helps rescue Mrs. Tully when she finds herself in a jam.

Gackenbach, Dick. *Dog for a Day*.

A second grader named Sidney invents a machine called a changing box. Sidney changes places with his dog, Wally, and winds up getting chased by a dogcatcher.

Laden, Nina. *The Night I Followed the Dog*.

Wondering where his dog goes at night, a boy follows the dog downtown to a night club named "The Doghouse."

Rylant, Cynthia. *Mr. Putter and Tabby Walk the Dog*.

When Mrs. Teaberry hurts her foot, Mr. Putter and his cat, Tabby, agree to walk Zeke, her dream "lollypup." Of course, Zeke turns out to be a nightmare.

ADDITIONAL POEMS

"My Dog He Is an Ugly Dog" by Jack Prelutsky from *The New Kid on the Block*.

"My Mother Doesn't Want a Dog" by Judith Viorst from *If I Were in Charge of the World*.

"The Puppy Chased the Sunbeam" by Ivy O. Eastwick from *Read-Aloud Rhymes for the Very Young*, edited by Jack Prelutsky.

"Rover" by Eve Merriam from *A Poem for a Pickle*.

"There Was a Small Dog Named Maggie," author unknown, from *Poems of A. Nonny Mouse*, edited by Jack Prelutsky.

ADDITIONAL SONGS AND
MUSICAL ACTIVITIES

"Bobo and Fred" by Rosenshontz from *Rock 'n' Roll Teddy Bear*.

"I Wanna Be a Dog" by Barry Louis Polisar from *Old Dog, New Tricks*.

"I've Got a Dog and His Name Is Cat" by Barry Louis Polisar from *Old Dog, New Tricks*.

"Rags" by Sharon, Lois and Bram from *Great Big Hits*.

"Rock and Roll Dog" from *Early Ears: Songs Just for 5 Year Olds*.

ADDITIONAL FINGERPLAYS AND MOVEMENT ACTIVITIES

"Frisky's Doghouse"
traditional

> This is Frisky's doghouse,
> *(Make a "roof" with fingers)*
> This is Frisky's bed.
> *(Hold out palm)*
> Here is Frisky's pan of milk,
> *(Cup hands)*
> So that she can be fed.
> *(Pretend to lap milk from cupped hands)*
> Frisky has a collar
> *(Circle neck with fingers)*
> With her tag upon it, too.
> *(Point to neck)*
> Take a stick and throw it,
> *(Motion of throwing stick)*
> She'll bring it back to you.
> *(Clap)*

"Puppies and Kittens"
traditional

> One little, two little, three little kittens
> *(Hold up three fingers)*
> Were napping in the sun.
> *(Place head on hands)*
> One little, two little, three little puppies
> *(Hold up three fingers on other hand)*
> Said, "Let's have some fun."

The puppies went sneaking
(Move the "puppy" fingers to the "kitten" fingers)
As quiet as could be.
One little, two little, three little kittens
Went scampering up a tree!
(Move "kitten" fingers up in the air)

VIDEOS

The Dog Who Had Kittens. Living Oak Media. (13 min.)
Martha Speaks. Reading Rainbow.

One Final Round
of Applause

I wrote this activity rhyme to celebrate audiences everywhere. My favorite audiences are those that attend Family Story-times. This is for them.

"A Round of Applause"
Rob Reid

You're so great!
Now please stand.
Give yourself
A great big hand.

Clap the floor.
Clap the chair.
Clap the wall
And clap the air.

Clap your elbows.
Clap your feet.
Clap your pinkies
And clap your seat.

Clap with flippers.
Clap with claws.
Now a big
Round of applause.

Clap your neighbor.
Don't ask how.
Last of all—
Take a bow!

Bibliography of Picture Books and Poems

Aardema, Verna. *Who's in Rabbit's House?* Illustrated by Leo and Diane Dillon. New York: Dial, 1977.

Ackerman, Karen. *Song and Dance Man.* Illustrated by Stephen Gammell. New York: Knopf, 1988.

Ada, Alma Flor. *Dear Peter Rabbit.* New York: Atheneum, 1994.

Adoff, Arnold. *Love Letters.* Illustrated by Lisa Desimini. New York: Blue Sky, 1997.

Ahlberg, Janet, and Allen Ahlberg. *The Jolly Postman and Other People's Letters.* Boston: Little, Brown, 1986.

Alarcon, Karen Beaumont. *Louella Mae, She's Run Away.* Illustrated by Rosanne Litzinger. New York: Henry Holt, 1997.

Alborough, Jez. *Where's My Teddy?* Cambridge, Mass.: Candlewick, 1992.

Alda, Arlene. *Sheep, Sheep, Sheep, Help Me Fall Asleep.* New York: Doubleday, 1992.

Andreae, Giles. *Rumble in the Jungle.* Illustrated by David Wojtowycz. London: Little Tiger, 1996.

Arnosky, Jim. *Every Autumn Comes the Bear.* New York: Putnam, 1993.

Asch, Frank. *Barnyard Lullaby.* New York: Simon and Schuster, 1998.

———. *Bread and Honey.* New York: Parents' Magazine, 1981.

———. *Just Like Daddy.* Englewood, N.J.: Prentice-Hall, 1981.

———. *Monkey Face.* New York: Parents' Magazine, 1977.

————. *Sand Cake.* New York: Parents' Magazine, 1978.

Ata, Te. *Baby Rattlesnake.* Illustrated by Veg Reisberg. San Francisco: Children's Book, 1989.

Aylesworth, Jim. *Old Black Fly.* Illustrated by Stephen Gammell. New York: Holt, 1991.

————. *Two Terrible Frights.* Illustrated by Eileen Christelow. New York: Atheneum, 1987.

Baltuck, Naomi. *Crazy Gibberish and Other Story Hour Stretches from a Storyteller's Bag of Tricks.* Hamden, Conn.: Linnet, 1993.

Bang, Molly. *The Paper Crane.* New York: Greenwillow, 1985.

Barnes-Murphy, Rowan. *Old MacDonald Had a Farm.* Woodbury, N.Y.: Barron's, 1985.

Barracca, Debra, and Sal Barracca. *The Adventures of Taxi Dog.* Illustrated by Mark Buehner. New York: Dial, 1990.

Barrett, Judi. *Animals Should Definitely Not Wear Clothing.* Illustrated by Ron Barrett. New York: Atheneum, 1984.

Bauer, Caroline Feller. *Leading Kids to Books through Magic.* Chicago: American Library Association, 1996.

————. *Midnight Snowman.* Illustrated by Catherine Stock. New York: Atheneum, 1987.

————. *Snowy Day: Stories and Poems.* Illustrated by Margot Tomes. New York: J. B. Lippincott, 1986.

Bierhorst, John. *On the Road of Stars: Native American Night Poems and Sleep Charms.* New York: Macmillan, 1994.

Birdseye, Tom. *Soap! Soap! Soap! Don't Forget the Soap!* Illustrated by Andrew Glass. New York: Holiday House, 1993.

Black, Charles C. *The Royal Nap.* Illustrated by James Stevenson. New York: Viking, 1995.

Bodecker, N. M. *Hurry, Hurry, Mary Dear and Other Nonsense Poems.* New York: Atheneum, 1976.

Brett, Jan. *The Hat.* New York: G. P. Putnam's Sons, 1997.

————. *The Mitten.* New York: G. P. Putnam's Sons, 1989.

Brown, Marc. *D.W. the Picky Eater.* Boston: Little, Brown, 1995.

Brown, Marcia. *Stone Soup.* New York: Scribner, 1947.

Brown, Margaret Wise. *Goodnight Moon.* Illustrated by Clement Hurd. New York: Harper, 1947.

————. *Little Donkey, Close Your Eyes.* Illustrated by Ashley Wolff. New York: HarperCollins, 1995.

————. *The Runaway Bunny.* Illustrated by Clement Hurd. New York: Harper and Row, 1942.

Bruchac, Joseph. *The Great Ball Game.* Illustrated by Susan Roth. New York: Dial, 1994.

Buckley, Helen E. *Grandmother and I.* Illustrated by Jan Omerod. New York: Lothrop, Lee and Shepard, 1994.

Bunting, Eve. *A Perfect Father's Day.* Illustrated by Susan Meddaugh. New York: Clarion, 1991.

Burton, Marilee Robin. *My Best Shoes.* Illustrated by James Ransome. New York: Tambourine, 1994.

Burton, Virginia Lee. *Mike Mulligan and His Steam Shovel.* Boston: Houghton Mifflin, 1939.

Butler, Dorothy. *My Brown Bear Barney.* Illustrated by Elizabeth Fuller. New York: Greenwillow, 1988.

Calmenson, Stephanie. *Never Take a Pig to Lunch.* Illustrated by Hilary Knight. Garden City, N.Y.: Doubleday, 1982.

————. *The Principal's New Clothes.* New York: Scholastic, 1989.

Caple, Kathy. *The Biggest Nose.* Boston: Houghton Mifflin, 1985.

Carle, Eric. *Eric Carle's Animals Animals.* New York: Philomel, 1989.

————. *The Grouchy Ladybug.* New York: Philomel, 1977.

————. *A House for Hermit Crab.* Saxonville, Mass.: Picture Book Studio, 1987.

————. *The Very Busy Spider.* New York: Philomel, 1984.

————. *The Very Hungry Caterpillar.* New York: Philomel, 1979.

————. *The Very Lonely Firefly.* New York: Philomel, 1995.

————. *The Very Quiet Cricket.* New York: Philomel, 1990.

Carlstrom, Nancy White. *Jesse Bear, What Will You Wear?* Illustrated by Bruce Degan. New York: Macmillan, 1986.

————. *Northern Lullaby.* Illustrated by Leo and Diane Dillon. New York: Philomel, 1992.

Carter, David A. *Alpha Bugs*. New York: Little Simon, 1994.

———. *How Many Bugs in a Box?* New York: Simon and Schuster, 1988.

———. *More Bugs in Boxes*. New York: Simon and Schuster, 1990.

Casey, Mike. *Red Lace, Yellow Lace*. Adapted by Judith Herbst. Illustrated by Jenny Stanley. Hauppauge, N.Y.: Barron's Educational Series, 1996.

Chapman, Cheryl. *Pass the Fritters, Critters*. New York: Four Winds, 1993.

Chevalier, Christa. *Spence Makes Circles*. Niles, Ill.: Albert Whitman, 1982.

Christelow, Eileen. *Five Little Monkeys Jumping on the Bed*. New York: Clarion, 1989.

Christiansen, Candace. *The Mitten Tree*. Illustrated by Elaine Greenstein. Golden, Colo.: Fulcrum Kids, 1997.

Cole, Joanna, ed. *It's Too Noisy*. Illustrated by Kate Duke. New York: Crowell, 1989.

———. *A New Treasury of Children's Poetry*. Illustrated by Judith Gwyn Brown. Garden City, N.Y.: Doubleday, 1984.

———. *Ready . . . Set . . . Read—and Laugh*. New York: Doubleday, 1995.

Cole, William, ed. *An Arkful of Animals*. Illustrated by Lynn Munsinger. Boston: Houghton Mifflin, 1978.

———. *Poem Stew*. Illustrated by Karen Weinhaus. New York: Lippincott, 1981.

———. *A Zooful of Animals*. Illustrated by Lynn Munsinger. Boston: Houghton Mifflin, 1992.

Corrin, Sara, and Stephen Corrin. *Once upon a Rhyme*. Illustrated by Jill Bennett. London: Farber and Farber, 1982.

Cowen, Catherine. *My Life with the Wave*. Illustrated by Mark Buehner. New York: Lothrop, Lee and Shepard, 1997.

Coy, John. *Night Driving*. Illustrated by Peter McCarty. New York: Henry Holt, 1996.

DePaola, Tomie. *Strega Nona*. Englewood Cliffs, N.J.: Prentice-Hall, 1975.

———. *Tomie DePaola's Book of Poems*. New York: Putnam, 1988.

De Regniers, Beatrice. *Sing a Song of Popcorn*. New York: Scholastic, 1988.

Duncan, Lois. *Songs from Dreamland*. New York: Knopf, 1989.

Dyer, Jane. *Animal Crackers: A Delectable Collection of Pictures, Poems, and Lullabies for the Very Young*. Boston: Little, Brown, 1994.

Eastman, P. D. *Are You My Mother?* New York: Random House, 1960.

Edwards, Richard. *Something's Coming!* Illustrated by Dana Kubrick. Cambridge, Mass.: Candlewick Press, 1995.

Ehlert, Lois. *Feathers for Lunch*. San Diego: Harcourt Brace Jovanovich, 1990.

———. *Fish Eyes*. San Diego: Harcourt Brace Jovanovich, 1990.

———. *Snowballs*. San Diego: Harcourt Brace Jovanovich, 1995.

Ehrlich, Amy. *Parents in the Pigpen, Pigs in the Tub*. Illustrated by Steven Kellogg. New York: Dial, 1993.

Emberley, Rebecca. *Three Cool Kids*. Boston: Little, Brown, 1995.

Emerson, Scott, and Howard Post. *The Magic Boots*. Layton, Utah: Gibbs-Smith, 1994.

Engel, Diana. *Josephina Hates Her Name*. New York: Morrow, 1989.

Ernst, Lisa Campbell. *Little Red Riding Hood: A Newfangled Prairie Tale*. New York: Simon and Schuster, 1995.

———. *The Rescue of Aunt Pansy*. New York: Viking Kestrel, 1987.

———. *Walter's Tail*. New York: Bradbury, 1992.

———. *When Bluebell Sang*. New York: Bradbury, 1981.

Evans, Katie. *Hunky Dory Ate It*. Illustrated by Janet Morgan Stoeke. New York: Dutton, 1992.

Evans, Lezlie. *Snow Dance*. Illustrated by Cynthia Jabar. Boston: Houghton Mifflin, 1997.

Fisher, Aileen. *Always Wondering: Some Favorite Poems of Aileen Fisher.* New York: HarperCollins, 1991.

———. *When It Comes to Bugs.* Illustrated by Chris and Bruce Degan. New York: Harper and Row, 1986.

Flack, Marjorie. *Ask Mr. Bear.* New York: Macmillan, 1932.

Fleischman, Paul. *Joyful Noise.* Illustrated by Eric Bedders. New York: Harper and Row, 1988.

Fleming, Denise. *Barnyard Banter.* New York: Henry Holt, 1994.

———. *Lunch.* New York: Henry Holt, 1992.

Florian, Doug. *Beast Feast.* San Diego: Harcourt Brace, 1994.

Fredericks, Anthony D. *Frantic Frogs and Other Frankly Fractured Folktales for Reader's Theatre.* Englewood, Colo.: Libraries Unlimited, 1993.

Gackenbach, Dick. *Dog for a Day.* New York: Clarion, 1987.

———. *Poppy the Panda.* New York: Clarion, 1984.

Gag, Wanda. *Millions of Cats.* New York: Coward-McCann, 1928.

Galdone, Paul. *Rumpelstiltskin.* New York: Clarion, 1985.

Gliori, Debi. *The Snowchild.* New York: Bradbury, 1994.

Goble, Paul. *Iktomi and the Boulder.* New York: Orchard, 1988.

Goldstein, Bobbye. *Bear in Mind: A Book of Bear Poems.* Illustrated by William Pene Du Bois. New York: Viking, 1989.

Gordon, Gaelyn. *Duckat.* Illustrated by Chris Gaskin. New York: Scholastic, 1992.

Guarrino, Deborah. *Is Your Mama a Llama?* Illustrated by Steven Kellogg. New York: Scholastic, 1989.

Gwynne, Fred. *Pondlarker.* New York: Simon and Schuster, 1990.

Hadithi, Mwenye. *Crafty Chameleon.* Illustrated by Adrienne Kennaway. Boston: Little, Brown, 1987.

———. *Hot Hippo.* Illustrated by Adrienne Kennaway. Boston: Little, Brown, 1986.

———. *Lazy Lion.* Illustrated by Adrienne Kennaway. Boston: Little, Brown, 1990.

Harley, Bill. *Sitting Down to Eat*. Illustrated by Kitty Harvill. Little Rock, Ark.: August House, 1996.

Harper, Isabelle, and Barry Moser. *My Cats Nick and Nora*. Illustrated by Barry Moser. New York: Blue Sky, 1995.

Hayes, Sarah. *Eat Up, Gemma*. Illustrated by Jan Ormerod. New York: Lothrop, Lee and Shepard, 1988.

———. *This Is the Bear*. Illustrated by Helen Craig. New York: Lippincott, 1986.

Henkes, Kevin. *Chrysanthemum*. New York: Greenwillow, 1991.

Hoberman, Mary Ann. *Fathers, Mothers, Sisters, Brothers: A Collection of Family Poems*. Illustrated by Marilyn Hafner. Boston: Joy Street Books, 1991.

———. *Yellow Butter, Purple Jelly, Red Jam, Black Bread*. Illustrated by Chaya Bernstein. New York: Viking, 1981.

Hong, Lily Tong. *Two of Everything*. Morton Grove, Ill.: Albert Whitman, 1993.

Hopkins, Lee Bennett. *Go to Bed: A Book of Bedtime Poems*. Illustrated by Rosekrans Hoffman. New York: Knopf, 1979.

———. *More Surprises*. Illustrated by Megan Lloyd. New York: Harper and Row, 1987.

———. *Side by Side: Poems to Read Together*. Illustrated by Hilary Knight. New York: Simon and Schuster, 1988.

———. *The Sky Is Full of Song*. New York: Harper and Row, 1983.

———. *Still As a Star: A Book of Nighttime Poems*. Illustrated by Karen Milone. Boston: Little, Brown, 1989.

———. *Surprises*. Illustrated by Megan Lloyd. New York: Harper and Row, 1984.

Hurwitz, Johanna. *New Shoes for Silvia*. Illustrated by Jerry Pinkney. New York: Morrow, 1993.

Jackson, Alison. *I Know an Old Lady Who Swallowed a Pie*. Illustrated by Judith Byron Schachner. New York: Dutton, 1997.

Janovitz, Marilyn. *Is It Time?* New York: North-South Books, 1994.

Johnson, Angela. *The Girl Who Wore Snakes.* Illustrated by James Ransome. New York: Orchard, 1993.

————. *Tell Me a Story, Mama.* Illustrated by David Soman. New York: Orchard, 1989.

Johnston, Tony. *Farmer Mack Measures His Pig.* Illustrated by Megan Lloyd. New York: Harper and Row, 1986.

Kallevig, Christina Petrell. *Folding Stories: Storytelling and Origami Together as One.* Newburgh, Ind.: Storytime Ink International, 1991.

Kasza, Keiko. *Grandpa Toad's Secrets.* New York: G. P. Putnam's Sons, 1995.

————. *The Wolf's Chicken Stew.* New York: G. P. Putnam's Sons, 1987.

Kennedy, X. J. *Ghastlies, Goops and Pincushions.* Illustrated by Ron Barrett. New York: Margaret K. McElderry, 1989.

Kennedy, X. J., and Dorothy M. Kennedy. *Talking Like the Rain: A First Book of Poems.* Boston: Little, Brown, 1992.

Kent, Jack. *The Caterpillar and the Polliwog.* New York: Prentice-Hall, 1982.

————. *Little Peep.* Englewood Cliffs, N.J.: Prentice-Hall, 1981.

————. *Round Robin.* Englewood Cliffs, N.J.: Prentice-Hall, 1987.

Keown, Elizabeth. *Emily's Snowball: The World's Biggest.* Illustrated by Irene Trivias. New York: Atheneum, 1992.

Kesey, Ken. *Little Tricker the Squirrel Meets Big Double the Bear.* Illustrated by Barry Moser. New York: Viking, 1990.

Kimmel, Eric. *Anansi and the Moss-Covered Rock.* Illustrated by Janet Stevens. New York: Holiday House, 1988.

King, P. E. *Down on the Funny Farm.* Illustrated by Alastair Graham. New York: Random House, 1986.

Knutson, Kimberley. *Bed Bouncers.* New York: Macmillan, 1995.

Krasilovsky, Phyllis. *The Man Who Didn't Wash His Dishes.* Illustrated by Barbara Cooney. Garden City, N.Y.: Doubleday, 1950.

Kraus, Robert. *Big Squeak, Little Squeak.* Illustrated by Kevin O'Malley. New York: Orchard Books, 1996.

————. *Milton, the Early Riser.* Illustrated by Jose Aruego and Ariene Dewey. New York: Simon and Schuster, 1972.

————. *Musical Max.* Illustrated by Jose Aruego and Ariene Dewey. New York: Simon and Schuster, 1990.

Kudrna, C. Imbrior. *To Bathe a Boa.* Minneapolis: Carolrhoda, 1986.

Laden, Nina. *The Night I Followed the Dog.* San Francisco: Chronicle Books, 1994.

Lansky, Bruce. *A Bad Case of the Giggles.* Illustrated by Stephen Carpenter. Deephaven, Minn.: Meadowbrook, 1994.

————. *Kids Pick the Funniest Poems.* Illustrated by Steve Carpenter. Deephaven, Minn.: Meadowbrook, 1991.

————. *The New Adventures of Mother Goose.* Illustrated by Stephen Carpenter. Deephaven, Minn.: Meadowbrook, 1993.

————. *You're Invited to Bruce Lansky's Poetry Party.* Illustrated by Stephen Carpenter. Deephaven, Minn.: Meadowbrook, 1996.

Larrick, Nancy. *Mice are Nice.* Illustrated by Ed Young. New York: Philomel, 1990.

————. *When the Dark Comes Dancing: a Bedtime Poetry Book.* Illustrated by John Wallner. New York: Philomel, 1983.

Leaf, Munro. *The Story of Ferdinand.* New York: Viking, 1936.

Lee, Dennis. *Alligator Pie.* Illustrated by Frank Newfeld. Boston: Houghton Mifflin, 1974.

————. *The Ice Cream Store.* Illustrated by David McPhail. New York: Scholastic, 1991.

————. *Garbage Delight.* Illustrated by Frank Newfeld. Boston: Houghton Mifflin, 1977.

Lester, Helen. *A Porcupine Named Fluffy.* Illustrated by Lynn Munsinger. Boston: Houghton Mifflin, 1985.

————. *Tacky the Penguin.* Illustrated by Lynn Munsinger. Boston: Houghton Mifflin, 1988.

————. *Three Cheers for Tacky.* Illustrated by Lynn Munsinger. Boston: Houghton Mifflin, 1994.

Lillie, Patricia. *When the Rooster Crowed.* Illustrated by Nancy Winslow Parker. New York: Greenwillow, 1991.

Lionni, Leo. *Cornelius.* New York: Pantheon, 1983.

———. *The Extraordinary Egg.* New York: Knopf, 1994.

———. *Six Crows.* New York: Knopf, 1988.

———. *Swimmy.* New York: Pantheon, 1963.

Livingston, Myra Cohen. *Poems for Grandmothers.* Illustrated by Patricia Cullen-Clark. New York: Holiday, 1990.

———. *Poems for Mothers.* Illustrated by Deborah Kogan Ray. New York: Holiday House. 1988.

Lobel, Arnold. *Whiskers and Rhymes.* New York: Greenwillow, 1985.

London, Jonathan. *Froggy Gets Dressed.* Illustrated by Frank Remkiewicz. New York: Viking, 1992.

———. *Let's Go Froggy!* Illustrated by Frank Remkiewicz. New York: Viking, 1994.

McBratney, Sam. *Guess How Much I Love You.* Illustrated by Anita Jeram. Cambridge, Mass.: Candlewick, 1995.

McCloskey, Robert. *Make Way for Ducklings.* New York: Viking, 1941.

McDermott, Gerald. *Coyote.* San Diego: Harcourt Brace Jovanovich, 1994.

———. *Zomo the Rabbit.* San Diego: Harcourt Brace Jovanovich, 1992.

MacDonald, Betty. *Mrs. Piggle Wiggle.* New York: Lippincott, 1947.

———. *Mrs. Piggle-Wiggle's Won't-Take-a-Bath-Cure.* Illustrated by Bruce Whatley. New York: HarperCollins, 1997.

MacDonald, Margaret Read. *Bookplay: 101 Creative Themes to Share with Young Children.* North Haven, Conn.: Library Professional Publications, 1995.

———. *Booksharing: 101 Program to Use with Preschoolers.* Hamden, Conn.: Library Professional Publications, 1988.

———. *Twenty Tellable Tales.* New York: Wilson, 1986.

McDonald, Megan. *Insects Are My Life.* Illustrated by Paul Brett Johnson. New York: Orchard, 1995.

MacDonald, Suse. *Peck Slither and Slide.* San Diego: Gullivar, 1997.

McMullen, Kate, and Lisa Eisenberg. *Buggy Riddles.* Illustrated by Simms Taback. New York: Dial, 1986.

Madden, Eric. *Curious Clownfish.* Illustrated by Adrienne Kennaway. Boston: Little, Brown, 1990.

Mahurin, Tim. *Jeremy Kooloo.* New York: Dutton, 1995.

Marshall, James. *Goldilocks and the Three Bears.* New York: Dial, 1988.

Marshall, Janet Perry. *My Camera: At the Aquarium.* Boston: Little, Brown, 1989.

Martin, Bill, Jr. *Chicka Chicka Boom Boom.* Illustrated by Lois Ehlert. New York: Simon and Schuster, 1989.

———. *The Happy Hippopotami.* Illustrated by Betsy Everitt. San Diego: Harcourt Brace Jovanovich, 1970, 1991.

Masurel, Claire. *Ten Dogs in the Window.* Illustrated by Pamela Paparone. New York: North-South, 1997.

Matthews, Judith, and Fay Robinson. *Nathaniel Willy, Scared Silly.* Illustrated by Alexi Natcheve. New York: Bradbury. 1993.

Mayer, Mercer. *Just Grandma and Me.* New York: Golden Press, 1983.

Meddaugh, Susan. *Martha Speaks.* Boston: Houghton Mifflin, 1992.

Merriam, Eve. *Blackberry Ink.* Illustrated by Hans Wilhelm. New York: Morrow, 1985.

———. *A Poem for a Pickle.* Illustrated by Sheila Hamanaka. New York: Morrow, 1989.

———. *You Be Good and I'll Be Night.* Illustrated by Karen Lee Schmidt. New York: Morrow, 1988.

Miller, Margaret. *Where Does It Go?* New York: Greenwillow, 1992.

———. *Whose Hat?* New York: Greenwillow, 1988.

———. *Whose Shoe?* New York: Greenwillow, 1991.

Miller, Sara Swan. *Three Stories You Can Read to Your Dog.* Illustrated by True Kelley. Boston: Houghton Mifflin, 1995.

Milne, A. A. *The House at Pooh Corner.* Illustrated by Ernest Shepard. New York: E. P. Dutton, 1927.

Minarik, Else Holmelund. *A Kiss for Little Bear.* Illustrated by Maurice Sendak. New York: Harper and Row, 1968.

Mosel, Arlene. *Tikki Tikki Tembo.* Illustrated by Blair Lent. New York: Holt, 1968.

Moss, Jeff. *The Butterfly Jar.* Illustrated by Chris Demarest. New York: Bantam Books, 1989.

———. *The Other Side of the Door.* Illustrated by Chris Demarest. New York: Bantam Books, 1991.

Most, Bernard. *A Dinosaur Named after Me.* San Diego: Harcourt Brace, 1991.

Munsch, Robert. *Mud Puddle.* Illustrated by Sami Suomalainen. Toronto: Annick, 1982, 1995.

———. *The Paper Bag Princess.* Illustrated by Michael Martchenko. Toronto: Annick, 1980.

———. *Thomas' Snowsuit.* Illustrated by Michael Martchenko. Toronto: Annick, 1985.

Murphy, Jill. *Five Minute's Peace.* New York: Putnam, 1986.

———. *Peace at Last.* New York: Dial, 1980.

Mwalimu and Adrienne Kennaway. *Awful Aardvaark.* Boston: Little, Brown, 1989.

Nash, Ogden. *Custard and Company.* Illustrated by Quentin Blake. Boston: Little, Brown, 1980.

Newman, Frederick. *Mouthsounds.* New York: Workman, 1980.

Nielsen, Laura F. *Jeremy's Muffler.* Illustrated by Christine M. Schneider. New York: Atheneum, 1995.

Nodset, Joan L. *Who Took the Farmer's Hat?* Illustrated by Fritz Siebel. New York: HarperCollins, 1963.

Novak, Matt. *Mouse TV.* New York: Orchard, 1994.

Numeroff, Laura Joffe. *If You Give a Mouse a Cookie.* Illustrated by Felicia Bond. New York: Harper and Row, 1985.

Oppenheim, Joanne. *You Can't Catch Me!* Illustrated by Andrew Shachat. Boston: Houghton Mifflin, 1986.

Palmer, Helen. *A Fish Out of Water.* Illustrated by P. D. Eastman. New York: Beginner Books, 1961.

Paulsen, Gary. *Puppies, Dogs, and Blue Northers: Reflections on Being Raised by a Pack of Sled Dogs.* San Diego: Harcourt Brace and Company, 1996.

Pellowski, Ann. *The Story Vine.* Illustrated by Lynn Sweat. New York: Macmillan, 1984.

Pfister, Marcus. *The Rainbow Fish.* New York: North-South, 1992.

Polacco, Patricia. *Thunder Cake.* New York: Philomel, 1990.

Pomerantz, Charlotte. *All Asleep.* Illustrated by Nancy Tafuri. New York: Greenwillow, 1984.

Porter, Sue. *Moose Music.* Racine, Wisc.: Western Publishing, 1994.

Poydar, Nancy. *Snip, Snip . . . Snow!* New York: Holiday House, 1997.

Prelutsky, Jack, ed. *For Laughing Out Loud.* Illustrated by Marjorie Priceman. New York: Knopf, 1991.

———. *For Laughing Out Louder.* Illustrated by Marjorie Priceman. New York: Knopf, 1995.

———. *The New Kid on the Block.* Illustrated by James Stevenson. New York: Greenwillow, 1984.

———. *A Pizza the Size of the Sun.* Illustrated by James Stevenson. New York: Greenwillow, 1996.

———. *Poems of A. Nonny Mouse.* Illustrated by Henrik Drescher. New York: Knopf, 1989.

———. *The Queen of Eene.* Illustrated by Victoria Chess. New York: Greenwillow, 1978.

———. *The Random House Book of Poetry for Children.* Illustrated by Arnold Lobel. New York: Random House, 1983.

———. *Read-Aloud Rhymes for the Very Young.* Illustrated by Marc Brown. New York: Knopf, 1986.

———. *Something Big Has Been Here.* Illustrated by James Stevenson. New York: Greenwillow, 1990.

Priceman, Marjorie. *How to Make an Apple Pie and See the World.* New York: Knopf, 1994.

Pringle, Laurence. *Naming the Cat.* Illustrated by Katherine Potter. New York: Walker, 1997.

————. *Octopus Hug*. Illustrated by Kate Salley Palmer. Honesdale, Pa.: Boyds Mill, 1993.

Pryor, Ainslie. *The Baby Blue Cat and the Dirty Dog Brothers*. New York: Viking Kestrel, 1987.

Pulver, Robin. *Mrs. Toggle's Zipper*. Illustrated by R. W. Alley. New York: Four Winds, 1990.

Radunsky, Eugenia, and Vladmir Radunsky. *Yucka Drucka Droni*. Illustrated by Vladmir Radunsky. New York: Scholastic, 1998.

Raffi. *Baby Beluga*. Illustrated by Ashley Wolff. New York: Crown, 1990.

————. *Spider on the Floor*. Illustrated by True Kelley. New York: Crown, 1993.

Reid, Rob. *Children's Jukebox: A Subject Guide to Musical Recordings and Programming Ideas for Songsters Ages One to Twelve*. Chicago: ALA, 1995.

————. *Wave Goodbye*. Illustrated by Lorraine Williams. New York: Lee and Low, 1996.

Reiser, Lynn. *Two Mice in Three Fables*. New York: Greenwillow, 1995.

Rogasky, Barbara. *Winter Poems*. Illustrated by Trina Schart Hyman. New York: Scholastic, 1994.

Rogers, Sally. *Earthsong*. Illustrated by Melissa Bay Mathis. New York: Dutton, 1998.

Roop, Peter, and Connie Roop. *Going Buggy*. Illustrated by Joan Hanson. Minneapolis: Lerner, 1986.

Rosen, Michael. *How Giraffe Got Such a Long Neck and Why Rhino Is So Grumpy*. Illustrated by John Clementson. New York: Dial, 1993.

————. *Poems for the Very Young*. Illustrated by Bob Graham. New York: Kingfisher Books, 1993.

————. *We're Going on a Bear Hunt*. Illustrated by Helen Oxenbury. New York: Margaret K. McElderry, 1989.

Rylant, Cynthia. *Henry and Mudge in Puddle Trouble*. Illustrated by Sucie Stevenson. New York: Bradbury, 1987.

————. *Mr. Putter and Tabby Walk the Dog*. Illustrated by Arthur Howard. San Diego: Harcourt Brace and Company, 1994.

Sadler, Marilyn. *Elizabeth and Larry*. Illustrated by Roger Bollen. London: Hamish Hamilton, 1990.

Schimmel, Nancy. *Just Enough to Make a Story*. 3d edition. Berkeley, Calif.: Sister's Choice, 1992.

Schwartz, Amy. *Bea and Mr. Jones*. Scarsdale, N.Y.: Bradbury, 1982.

Scieszka, Jon. *The Frog Prince Continued*. Illustrated by Steve Johnson. New York: Viking, 1991.

———. *The True Story of the Three Little Pigs*. Illustrated by Lane Smith. New York: Viking, 1989.

Serfozo, Mary. *Benjamin Bigfoot*. Illustrated by Jos A. Smith. New York: Margaret K. McElderry Books, 1993.

Seuss, Dr. *The Cat in the Hat*. New York: Random House, 1957.

———. *McElligot's Pool*. New York: Random House, 1947.

———. *The Sneetches and Other Stories*. New York: Random House, 1961.

Seymour, Tres. *Too Quiet for These Old Bones*. Illustrated by Paul Brett Johnson. New York: Orchard, 1997.

Shapiro, Arnold. *Mice Squeak, We Speak*. Illustrated by Tomie DePaola. New York: Putnam, 1997.

Sharmat, Mitchell. *Gregory, the Terrible Eater*. Illustrated by Jose Aruego and Ariene Dewey. New York: Four Winds, 1980.

Sharrat, Nick. *My Mom and Dad Make Me Laugh*. Cambridge, Mass.: Candlewick 1994.

Shaw, Nancy. *Sheep in a Jeep*. Illustrated by Margot Apple. Boston: Houghton Mifflin, 1986.

———. *Sheep Out to Eat*. Illustrated by Margot Apple. Boston: Houghton Mifflin, 1992.

Sierra Judy. *Counting Crocodiles*. San Diego: Harcourt Brace, 1997.

———. *The Flannel Board Storytelling Book*. New York: H. W. Wilson, 1987.

Silverstein, Shel. *Falling Up*. New York: HarperCollins, 1996.

———. *A Light in the Attic*. New York: HarperCollins, 1981.

———. *Where the Sidewalk Ends*. New York: Harper and Row, 1974.

————. *Who Wants a Cheap Rhinoceros?* New York: Macmillan, 1964, 1983.

Singer, Marilyn. *Turtle in July.* Illustrated by Jerry Pinkney. New York: Macmillan, 1989.

Slate, Joseph. *Miss Bindergarten Gets Ready for Kindergarten.* Illustrated by Ashley Wolff. New York: Dutton, 1996.

Sloat, Teri. *The Thing That Bothered Farmer Brown.* Illustrated by Nadine Bernard Westcott. New York: Orchard, 1995.

Slobodkina, Esphyr. *Caps for Sale.* Reading, Mass.: Young, Scott, 1947.

Small, David. *Fenwick's Suit.* New York: Farrar, Straus, Giroux, 1996.

Smith, William Jay. *Ho for a Hat!* Illustrated by Lynn Munsinger. Boston: Little, Brown, 1964, 1989.

Soto, Gary. *Chato's Kitchen.* Illustrated by Susan Guevara. New York: Putnam's, 1995.

Steig, William. *Doctor De Soto.* New York: Farrar, Straus and Giroux, 1982.

Steptoe, Javaka. *In Daddy's Arms, I Am Tall.* New York: Lee and Low, 1997.

Stevens, Janet. *Tops and Bottoms.* San Diego: Harcourt Brace Jovanovich, 1995.

————. *The Tortoise and the Hare.* New York: Holiday House, 1984.

Stoeke, Janet Morgan. *A Hat for Minerva Louise.* New York: Dutton, 1994.

Sutherland, Harry A. *Dad's Car Wash.* New York: Atheneum, 1988.

Temko, Florence. *Paper Pandas and Jumping Frogs.* San Francisco: China Books, 1986.

Thaler, Mike. *What Could a Hippopotamus Be?* New York: Simon and Schuster, 1975, 1990.

Thomas, Patricia. *"Stand Back," Said the Elephant, "I'm Going to Sneeze!"* Illustrated by Wallace Tripp. New York: Lothrop, Lee and Shepard, 1971, 1990.

Tolhurst, Marilyn. *Somebody and the Three Blairs.* New York: Orchard, 1990.

Torres, Leyla. *Saturday Sancocho*. New York: Farrar, Straus, Giroux, 1995.

Trivizas, Eugene. *The Three Little Wolves and the Big Bad Pig*. Illustrated by Helen Oxenbury. New York: Margaret K. McElderry, 1993.

Van Laan, Nancy. *This Is the Hat*. Illustrated by Holly Meade. Boston: Little, Brown, 1992.

Vaughn, Marcia. *Wombat Stew*. Illustrated by Pamela Lofts. Englewood Cliffs, N.J.: Silver Burdett, 1984.

Viorst, Judith. *If I Were in Charge of the World*. Illustrated by Lynn Cherry. New York: Atheneum, 1981.

———. *Sad Underwear and Other Complications*. Illustrated by Richard Hull. New York: Atheneum, 1995.

Vozar, David. *Yo! Hungry Wolf*. New York: Doubleday, 1993.

Waber, Bernard. *Bearsie Bear and the Surprise Sleepover Party*. Boston: Houghton Mifflin, 1997.

Waddell, Martin. *Farmer Duck*. Illustrated by Helen Oxenbury. Cambridge, Mass.: Candlewick, 1991.

———. *Little Mo*. Illustrated by Jill Barton. Cambridge, Mass.: Candlewick, 1993.

Wahl, Jan. *Cats and Robbers*. Illustrated by Dolores Avendano. New York: Tambourine, 1995.

Walsh, Ellen Stoll. *Mouse Count*. San Diego: Harcourt Brace Jovanovich, 1991.

———. *Mouse Paint*. San Diego: Harcourt Brace Jovanovich, 1989.

Ward, Helen. *The King of the Birds*. Brookfield, Conn.: Millbrook, 1997.

Warren, Jean. *1-2-3 Colors: Colorful Activities for Young Children*. Illustrated by Marion Hopping Ekberg. Everett, Wash.: Warren, 1988.

Watanabe, Shigeo. *How Do I Put It On?* Illustrated by Yasuo Ohtomo. New York: Philomel, 1977.

———. *I Can Take a Bath*. Illustrated by Yasuo Ohtomo. New York: Philomel, 1986.

Wiesner, David. *Tuesday*. New York: Clarion, 1991.

Wildsmith, Brian, and Rebecca Wildsmith. *Wake Up, Wake Up*. San Diego: Harcourt Brace Jovanovich, 1993.

Wilmes, Liz, and Dick Wilmes. *Felt Board Fun*. Illustrated by Donna Dane. Elgin, Ill.: Building Blocks, 1984.

Wolf, Jake. *What You Do Is Easy, What I Do Is Hard*. Illustrated by Ann Dewdney. New York: Greenwillow, 1996.

Wolff, Patricia Rae. *The Toll Bridge Troll*. Illustrated by Kimberly Bucken Root. San Diego: Browndeer, 1995.

Wood, Audrey. *Birdsong*. Illustrated by Robert Florczak. San Diego: Harcourt Brace Jovanovich, 1997.

———. *King Bidgood's in the Bathtub*. Illustrated by Don Wood. San Diego: Harcourt Brace Jovanovich, 1985.

———. *The Napping House*. Illustrated by Don Wood. San Diego: Harcourt Brace Jovanovich, 1984.

———. *Silly Sally*. San Diego: Harcourt Brace Jovanovich, 1992.

Wood, Audrey, and Don Wood. *The Little Mouse, the Red Ripe Strawberry, and the Big Hungry Bear*. Illustrated by Don Wood. New York: Child's Play, 1984, 1993.

Wynot, Jillian. *The Mother's Day Sandwich*. Illustrated by Maxie Chambliss. New York: Orchard, 1990.

Yolen, Jane. *Owl Moon*. Illustrated by John Schoenherr. New York: Philomel, 1987.

———. *The Three Bears Rhyme Book*. Illustrated by Jane Dyer. San Diego: Harcourt Brace Jovanovich, 1987.

Young, Ed. *Seven Blind Mice*. New York: Philomel, 1992.

Zion, Gene. *Harry the Dirty Dog*. New York: Harper, 1956.

Zolotow, Charlotte. *The Quiet Mother and the Noisy Little Boy*. Illustrated by Marc Simont. New York: Harper and Row, 1953, 1989.

———. *This Quiet Lady*. Illustrated by Anita Lobel. New York: Greenwillow, 1992.

Discography of Songs and Tunes

Alsop, Peter. *Wha'd'ya Wanna Do?* Moose School Productions, 1983.

Arnold, Linda. *Happiness Cake.* A & M Records, 1989.

———. *Make Believe.* A & M Records, 1986.

———. *Sing Along Stew.* A & M Records, 1995.

Avni, Fran. *Artichokes and Brussel Sprouts.* Lemonstone Records, 1988.

Ballingham, Pamela. *A Treasury of Earth Mother Lullabies.* Earth Mother Productions, 1990.

Baltuck, Naomi. *Crazy Gibberish.* Naomi Baltuck, 1993.

Banana Slug String Band. *Dirt Made My Lunch.* Music for Little People, 1989.

———. *Slugs at Sea.* Music for Little People, 1991.

Bartels, Joanie. *Bathtime Magic.* Discovery Music, 1989.

———. *Sillytime Magic.* Discovery Music, 1989.

Bishop, Heather. *Bellybutton.* Mother of Pearl Records, 1982.

Buchman, Rachel. *Hello Everybody.* A Gentle Wind, 1986.

———. *Hello Rachel! Hello Children!* Rounder Records, 1988.

———. *Sing a Song of Seasons.* Rounder Records, 1997.

Cappelli, Frank. *Take a Seat.* A & M Records, 1993.

Carfra, Pat. *Babes, Beasts and Birds.* Lullaby Productions, 1987.

Cassidy, Nancy. *Kids' Songs.* Klutz Press, 1986.

———. *Kids' Songs 2.* Klutz Press, 1989.

Chapin, Tom. *Billy the Squid.* Sony, 1992.

————. *Family Tree*. Sony, 1988.

————. *Moonboat*. Sony, 1989.

————. *Mother Earth*. Sony, 1990.

————. *Zag Zig*. Sony, 1994.

Charette, Rick. *Alligator in the Elevator*. Pine Point Records, 1985.

————. *Chickens on Vacation*. Pine Point Records, 1990.

————. *Where Do My Sneakers Go at Night?* Pine Point Records, 1987.

The Chenille Sisters. *The Big Picture*. Red House Records, 1992.

————. *1-2-3 for Kids*. Red House Records, 1989.

The Civil War: Original Soundtrack Recording. Elektra Nonesuch, 1990.

Colleen and Uncle Squaty. *Colleen and Uncle Squaty*. Hannafin/Woody, 1993.

Diamond, Charlotte. *10 Carrot Diamond*. Hug Bug Records, 1985.

Early Ears: Songs Just for 5 Year Olds. ZOOM Express, 1992.

Feinstein, Michael. *Pure Imagination*. Elektra, 1992.

Fink, Cathy. *Grandma Slid Down the Mountain*. Rounder Records, 1987.

Fink, Cathy, and Marcy Marxer. *A Cathy and Marcy Collection for Kids*. Rounder Records, 1994.

————. *Help Yourself*. Rounder Records, 1990.

Garcia, Jerry, and David Grissman. *Not for Kids Only*. Acoustic Disc, 1993.

Glazer, Tom. *Children's Greatest Hits*. CMS Records, 1977.

Grammer, Red. *Can You Sound Just Like Me?* Smilin' Atcha Music, 1983.

————. *Down the Do-Re-Mi*. Smilin' Atcha Music, 1991.

Grandma's Patchwork Quilt. American Melody, 1987.

Greg and Steve. *Kidding Around*. Youngheart Records, 1985.

————. *Kids in Motion*. Youngheart Records, 1987.

————. *Playing Favorites*. Youngheart Records, 1991.

————. *We All Live Together, Vol. 1*. Youngheart Records, 1975.

————. *We All Live Together, Vol. 4*. Youngheart Records, 1980.

————. *We All Live Together, Vol. 5*. Youngheart Records, 1994.

Grunsky, Jack. *Jumpin' Jack*. BMG, 1996.

Guthrie, Woody. *Woody's 20 Grow Big Songs*. Warner Brothers, 1992.

Harley, Bill. *Come on Out and Play*. Round River Records, 1990.

————. *Monsters in the Bathroom*. Round River Records, 1984.

Harper, Jessica. *40 Winks*. Alacazam, 1998.

Harper, Monty. *Imagine That*. Monty Harper Productions, 1996.

Herdman, Priscilla. *Stardreamer*. Music for Little People, 1988.

Ives, Burl. *The Little White Duck*. MCA Records, 1974.

Kahn, Si. *Good Times and Bed Times*. Rounder Records, 1993.

Lewis, Shari. *Lamb Chop's Sing-Along, Play-Along*. A & M, 1988.

Little Richard. *Shake It All About*. Disney, 1992.

McCutcheon, John. *Family Garden*. Rounder Records, 1993.

————. *Howjadoo*. Rounder Records, 1987.

————. *Mail Myself to You*. Rounder Records, 1988.

————. *Wintersongs*. Rounder Records, 1995.

McGrath, Bob, and Katherine Smithrim. *Songs and Games for Toddlers*. Kids' Records, 1985.

Mancini, Henry. *All Time Greatest Hits*. RCA, 1988.

Marxer, Marcy. *Jump Children*. Rounder Records, 1986.

Mattox, Cheryl Warren. *Shake It to the One That You Love the Best: Play Songs and Lullabies from Black Musical Traditions*. Warren-Mattox Productions, 1989.

Mayer, Hans. *See Ya Later, Alligator*. Myther Records, 1997.

Moo, Anna. *Anna Moo Cracker*. A. Moosic Productions, 1994.

Nagler, Eric. *Improvise with Eric Nagler*. Rounder Records, 1989.

O'Brien, Bruce. *Love Is in the Middle*. Tomorrow River, 1995.

Palmer, Hap. *Peek-a-Boo*. Hap-Pal Music, 1990.

Parachute Express. *Happy to Be Here*. Disney, 1991.

Paxton, Tom. *Goin' to the Zoo*. Rounder Records, 1977.

———. *I've Got a Yo-Yo*. Rounder Records, 1997.

Peanut Butter and Jelly. *Peanut Butter and Jelly's Greatest Hits*. Tom Knight Productions, 1995.

Peanutbutterjam. *Incredibly Spreadable*. Peanutbutterjam, 1984.

———. *Simply Singable*. Peanutbutterjam, 1988.

Penner, Fred. *Collections*. Oak Street Music, 1989.

———. *Ebeneezer Sneezer*. Oak Street Music, 1991.

———. *Happy Feet*. Oak Street Music, 1992.

Peter, Paul and Mary. *Peter, Paul and Mommy*. Warner Brothers, n.d.

———. *Peter, Paul and Mommy, Too*. Warner Brothers, 1993.

Phipps, Bonnie. *Dinosaur Choir*. Wimmer-Ferguson, 1992.

———. *Monsters' Holiday*. Wimmer-Ferguson, 1994.

Polisar, Barry Louis. *Family Concert*. Rainbow Morning Music, 1990.

———. *Old Dog, New Tricks*. Rainbow Morning Music, 1993.

———. *Teacher's Favorites*. Rainbow Morning Music, 1993.

Queen. *Greatest Hits*. Hollywood Records, 1992.

Raffi. *Baby Beluga*. Troubadour, 1977.

———. *Corner Grocery Store*. Troubadour, 1979.

———. *Everything Grows*. Troubadour, 1987.

———. *One Light, One Sun*. Troubadour, 1982.

———. *Raffi in Concert with the Rise and Shine Band*. Troubadour, 1989.

———. *Rise and Shine*. Troubadour, 1982.

———. *Singable Songs for the Very Young*. Troubadour, 1976.

Robertson, Mae, and Don Jackson. *All through the Night*. Lyric Partners, 1994.

Rogers, Sally. *Piggyback Planet*. Round River Records, 1992.

———. *What Can One Little Person Do?* Round River Records, 1990.

Ronstadt, Linda. *Dedicated to the One I Love*. Elektra, 1996.

Rosen, Gary. *Tot Rock.* Lightyear, 1993.

Rosenshontz. *Family Vacation.* Lightyear, 1988.

———. *It's the Truth.* Lightyear, 1984.

———. *Rock and Roll Teddy Bear.* Lightyear, 1986.

———. *Rosenshontz Tickles You.* Lightyear, 1980.

———. *Share It.* Lightyear, 1982.

———. *Uh-Oh.* Lightyear, 1990.

Roth, Kevin. *Oscar, Bingo and Buddies.* Marlboro Records, 1986.

———. *Travel Song Sing Alongs.* Marlboro Records, 1994.

———. *Unbearable Bears.* Marlboro Records, 1986.

Sapp, Jane. *We've All Got Stories.* Rounder Records, 1996.

Scruggs, Joe. *Ants.* Educational Graphics Press, 1994.

———. *Bahamas Pajamas.* Educational Graphics Press, 1990.

———. *Deep in the Jungle.* Educational Graphics Press, 1987.

———. *Even Trolls Have Moms.* Educational Graphics Press, 1988.

———. *Late Last Night.* Educational Graphics Press, 1984.

Seeger, Pete. *Abiyoyo and Other Story Songs for Children.* Smithsonian/Folkways, 1989.

———. *Stories and Songs for Little Children.* High Windy Audio, n.d.

Sesame Street. *Jim Henson: A Sesame Street Celebration.* Sony, 1991.

———. *Splish Splash: Bath Time Fun.* Sony, 1995.

Sharon, Lois and Bram. *All the Fun You Can Sing.* Elephant Records, 1992.

———. *Elephant Party.* Drive, 1996.

———. *The Elephant Show Record.* Elephant Records, 1986.

———. *Great Big Hits.* Elephant Records, 1992.

———. *Mainly Mother Goose.* Elephant Records, 1984.

———. *One Elephant.* Elephant Records, 1980.

———. *One, Two, Three, Four, Live!* Elephant Records, 1982.

————. *Sing A to Z*. Elephant Records, 1990.

————. *Singing 'n' Swinging*. Elephant Records, 1980.

————. *Smorgasbord*. Elephant Records, 1980.

————. *Stay Tuned*. Elephant Records, 1987.

Shontz, Bill. *Animal Tales*. Lightyear, 1993.

————. *Teddy Bear's Greatest Hits*. Lightyear, 1997.

Staines, Bill. *The Happy Wanderer*. Red House Records, 1993.

Tickle Tune Typhoon. *Circle Around*. Tickle Tune Typhoon, 1983.

————. *Hug the Earth*. Tickle Tune Typhoon, 1985.

Tillery, Linda. *Shakin' a Tailfeather*. Music for Little People, 1997.

Troubadour. *On the Trail*. A Gentle Wind, 1990.

Walker, Mary Lu. *The Frog's Party*. A Gentle Wind, 1989.

Wee Sing. Price Stern Sloan, 1977.

Wee Sing and Play. Price Stern Sloan, 1986.

Wee Sing Fun 'n' Folk. Price Stern Sloan, 1989.

Wee Sing Silly Songs. Price Stern Sloan, 1986.

Index of Titles

Abiyoyo and Other Story Songs for Children (recording), 56, 61, 93

About the Teeth of Sharks, 172

Adventures of Taxi Dog, The, 211

After a Bath, 63

All God's Critters, 192

All Kinds of Grands, 144

All the Fun You Can Sing (recording), 121

All through the Night (recording), 91

All Time Greatest Hits (recording), 42

Alligator, The, 85

Alligator in the Elevator (recording), 67

Alligator Pie, 81, 156

Alligator Stomp, 82

Always Be Kind to Animals, 192

Always My Dad (video), 138

Anansi, 157

Anansi and the Moss-Covered Rock, 150

Anansi and the Moss-Covered Rock (video), 76

Anansi Goes Fishing (video), 86

And After a Hundred Years Had Passed, Sleeping Beauty Awoke (at Last!) from Her Slumber, 26

And Then the Prince Knelt Down and Tried to Put the Glass Slipper on Cinderella's Foot, 26

Animal Crackers: A Delightful Collection of Pictures, Poems, and Lullabies for the Very Young, 34

Animal Sounds in Different Languages, 192–3

Animal Tales (recording), 197

Animals Should Definitely Not Wear Clothing, 178

Ants (recording), 75

Ants Go Marching, The, 75

Ants in My Pants, 164

Apples and Bananas/Lima Beans and Diced Beets, 183–4

Are You My Mother?, 51

Arkful of Animals, An, 60, 61

Artichokes and Brussel Sprouts (recording), 75, 205

As I Was Going to St. Ives, 96–7

As I Was Walking Round the Lake, 85

Ask Mr. Bear, 144

Aunt Samantha, 129

Awful Aardvaark, 92

B-I-N-G-O, 210

Babes, Beasts, and Birds (recording), 29, 32

Baby Beluga, 169

Baby Beluga (recording), 30, 189

Baby Bird, 164

Baby Blue Cat and the Dirty Dog Brothers, The, 66

Baby Chick, 33

Baby Elephant Walk, 42
Baby Rattlesnake, 84
Baby Rhinoceros, A, 37
Bad Case of the Giggles, A, 93, 124, 129, 136, 179
Bahamas Pajamas (recording), 52
Balloons, 164
Band-Aids, 161
Barn Owl, 52
Barnyard Banter, 29
Barnyard Dance, 34
Barnyard Lullaby, 32
Bat, The, 196
Bathtime, 67
Bathtime Magic (recording), 67
Be Kind to Your Parents, 15, 137
Bea and Mr. Jones, 136
Bea and Mr. Jones (video), 138
Beady Bear (video), 61
Bear Hunt, 57–9
Bear in Mind: A Book of Bear Poems, 61
Bear in There, 59
Bear That Snores, The, 61, 93
Bear Went over the Mountain, The, 61
Bears, 60
Bearsie Bear and the Surprise Sleepover Party, 192
Beast Feast, 52, 196
Bed Bouncers, 92
Bedtime, 92
Bedtime Round, 93
Before I Jump into Bed, 129–30
Benjamin Bigfoot, 126
Bernard, 115
Bertie Bertie, 67
Best Old Hat, The, 129
Big Old Cat, 99
Big Picture, The (recording), 114
Big Squeak, Little Squeak, 120
Biggest Nose, The, 38
Billy Magee Magaw, 47–8
Billy the Squid (recording), 56, 61, 93

Birdseed, 52
Birdsong, 47
Biscuits in the Oven, 189
Black Socks, 127
Blackberry Ink, 67
Blueberries for Sal (video), 146
Boa Constrictor, 85
Bobo and Fred, 212
Bookplay: 101 Creative Themes to Share with Young Children, 1
Booksharing: 101 Programs to Use with Preschoolers, 1
Boom, Bang, 111
Boom, Boom, Ain't It Great to Be Crazy, 164
Brave Irene (video), 206
Bread and Honey, 140
Bubble Bath, 67
Bug, 74
Buggy Riddles, 70
Burt Dow: Deep-Water Man (video), 173
Busy Day, 93–4
Butts Up, 52

Can You Growl Like a Tiger?, 193
Can You Sound Just Like Me? (recording), 110
Caps for Sale, 125
Caps for Sale (video), 130
Cat Bath, 101
Cat Came Back, The, 101
Cat in the Hat, The, 163
Cat Kisses, 101
Caterpillar and the Polliwog, The, 71
Caterpillar and the Polliwog, The (video), 76
Cathy and Marcy Collection for Kids, A (recording), 31, 85
Cats, 96
Cats and Robbers, 100
Charlie Needs a Cloak (video), 181
Chato's Kitchen, 96
Chester, 122

Chicka Chicka Boom Boom,
160
Chicken Little (video), 165
Chickens on Vacation (recording), 56, 61, 93
Children's Greatest Hits (recording), 14
Children's Jukebox: A Subject Guide to Musical Recordings and Programming Ideas for Songsters Ages One to Twelve,
5, 6
Choose an Author, 148
Chrysanthemum, 114
Chrysanthemum (video), 122
Circle Around (recording), 129
Circus Baby, The (video), 45
Civil War, The: Original Soundtrack Recording, 47
Clatter, 109
Clean Gene, 67
Closet Full of Shoes, A, 129
Cloudy with a Chance of Meatballs (video), 190
Cluck, Cluck, Red Hen, 34
Collections (recording), 44, 101
Colleen and Uncle Squaty (recording), 78
Corduroy (video), 61
Cornelius, 84
Corner Grocery Store (recording), 34, 157, 183
Counting Crocodiles, 84
Coyote, 156
Crafty Chameleon, 84
Crazy Traffic Light, The, 107–8
Cricket Song, The, 75
Crickets, 74
Criss-Cross Applesauce, 5
Crocodile's Toothache, The, 82
Crow That Wanted to Sing, The, 52
Curious Clownfish, 168
Custard and Company, 52, 197

D. W. the Picky Eater, 188
Daddy Does the Dishes, 137

Dad's Car Wash, 64
Dad's Got That Look, 137
Dainty Dottie Dee, 67
Day Jimmy's Boa Ate the Wash, The (video), 35
Dear Hard Working Dad, 136
Dear Peter Rabbit, 25
Dedicated to the One I Love (recording), 91
Deep in the Jungle (recording), 197
Did You Feed My Cow?, 34
Dimpleton the Simpleton, 33
Dincerella, 22–4
Dinosaur Choir (recording), 189
Dinosaur Named after Me, A, 120
Dirt Made My Lunch (recording), 85
Do Your Ears Hang Low?, 209
Doctor De Soto, 149
Doctor De Soto (video), 157
Dog for a Day, 212
Dog Who Had Kittens, The (video), 214
Don't Be Rude to a Rhinoceros, 43
Don't Trick Your Dad, 132
Dora Diller, 71
Down on Grandpa's Farm, 31–2
Down on the Farm, 29
Down on the Funny Farm, 33
Down the Do-Re-Mi (recording), 34, 192
Dressing Song, The, 179
Duck, The, 52
Duckat, 49

E, I, Addie Addie, O, 157
Early Bird, 52
Early Ears: Songs Just for 5 Year Olds (recording), 213
Earth Mother recordings, 91
Earthsong, 196
Eat Up, Gemma, 188
Ebeneezer Sneezer (recording), 164

Eddie Coochie, 115–16
Eensy Weensy Spider, The, 73
Elephant Goes Like This and That, An, 38–9
Elephant Hunt, 39–42
Elephant Is Hard to Hide, An, 43
Elephant Party (recording), 121, 179
Elephant Riddles, 37
Elephant Show Record, The (recording), 24, 89
Elizabeth and Larry, 84
Emily's Snowball: The World's Biggest, 204
Englebert the Elephant, 43
Eric Carle's Animals Animals, 33, 34, 43, 52, 75, 196
Even Trolls Have Moms (recording), 26
Every Autumn Comes the Bear, 60
Everybody Eats When They Come to My House, 121
Everybody's Got to Have a Home, 197
Everything Grows (recording), 67
Exploding Frog, The, 82–84
Extraordinary Egg, 81
Eye Winker, Tom Tinker, Chin Chopper, 116

Falling Up, 67, 110, 129, 156, 204
Family Concert (recording), 145
Family Garden (recording), 15, 137, 189
Family Tree (recording), 157
Family Vacation (recording), 15, 137
Farm Is in a Flurry, The, 30, 110
Farmer and the Queen, The, 34
Farmer Duck, 31
Farmer Mack Measures His Pig, 33

Fathers, Mothers, Sisters, Brothers: A Collection of Family Poems, 136, 144, 179
Fearsome Beast, The, 38
Feathers for Lunch, 51
Felt Board Fun, 78
Fenwick's Suit, 178
Fish, 172
Fish Eyes, 171
Fish Out of Water, A, 13–14
Five Frogs, 80
Five Little Birdies, 53
Five Little Ducks, 49–50, 142–3
Five Little Frogs, 80
Five Little Kittens, 102
Five Little Mice, 97–8, 102
Five Little Monkeys, 197
Five Little Monkeys Jumping on the Bed, 161
Five Little Snowmen, 205–6
Five Minute's Peace, 64
Five Plump Peas, 189–90
Flea, Fly, Mosquito, 75
Flyaway Pantloons, The (video), 181
Flying 'Round the Mountain, 26
Folding Stories: Storytelling and Origami Together as One, 130
Foolish Frog, The, 85
For Each a Hat, 130
For Laughing Out Loud, 26, 52, 121, 172, 189
For Laughing Out Louder, 197
Forty Winks (recording), 91
Four Generations, 136
Frantic Frogs and Other Frankly Fractured Folktales for Readers' Theatre, 24
Freeze, The, 157
Friendly Frederick Fuddlestone, 121
Frisky's Doghouse, 213
Frog, 85
Frog and Toad Together (video), 86
Frog Goes to Dinner (video), 86, 190
Frog on the Log, The, 85

Frog Prince Continued, The, 25
Froggy Choir, The, 79–80
Froggy Gets Dressed, 176
Frog's Party, The (recording),
    75, 205
Furry Bear, 61
Fuzzy Wuzzy, 56
Fuzzy Wuzzy, Creepy Crawly,
    75

Garbage Delight, 67
Giraffes, 196
Girl Who Wore Snakes, The, 84
Gned the Gnu, 197
*Go to Bed: A Book of Bedtime
    Poems,* 92
Goin' to the Zoo (recording),
    43, 197
Going Buggy, 70
Goldilocks and the Three Bears,
    56
Goldilocks and the Three Bears
    (video), 27
Goldilocks Rap, 26
Good Times and Bed Times
    (recording), 88
Goodnight Moon, 14
Grand Old Duke of York, The,
    151–2
*Grandma Slid Down the
    Mountain* (recording), 26,
    145
Grandma's Glasses, 145
Grandma's Lullaby, 143
Grandma's Patchwork Quilt
    (recording), 81, 145
Grandmother and I, 143
Grandpa McWheeze, 136
Grandpa Toad's Secrets, 132
Grandpa's Whiskers, 132
Grasshopper, The, 165
Great Ball Game, The, 193
Great Big Hits (recording), 31,
    44, 73, 101, 211, 212
*Great White Man-Eating Shark,
    The* (video), 173
Greatest Hits (recording), 105
Gregory, the Terrible Eater, 188

Grizzly Bear, 61
Grouchy Ladybug, The, 74
Guess How Much I Love You,
    133
Guess the Headlines, 150
Guess the Nursery Rhyme, 149

Halfway Down, 16
Hand Jive, 107
Hand-Me-Downs, 179
Handiest Nose, The, 43
Hands on Shoulders, 12
Happiness Cake (recording), 44
Happy Birthday, Mother
    Dearest, 144
Happy Feet (recording), 129
Happy Hippo, The, 42
Happy to Be Here (recording),
    179–80
Happy Wanderer, The (record-
    ing), 192
Harry the Dirty Dog, 66
Harry the Dirty Dog (video), 68
Hat, The, 200
Hat, The (video), 130
Hat for Minerva Louise, A, 128
Head, Shoulders, Knees, and
    Toes, 64–5
Heading on Down to the Barn,
    34
Headphone Harold, 110
Hello, 5
Hello Everybody (recording),
    32, 49
Hello Ladybug, 75
Helping Daddy, 137
*Henry and Mudge in Puddle
    Trouble,* 163
Here Comes the Cat (video), 103
Here Is the Beehive, 75–6
Here We Go Loop 'D Loo, 16,
    65–6, 117
Here We Go Round the
    Mulberry Bush, 176
Here's a Great Big Hill, 206
Hibernation, 200
Hickory Dickory Dock, 21, 101
Hippo Hooray, 44

Hippopotamus, 43
Hippopotamus Rock, 44
Ho for a Hat!, 124
Hokey Pokey, The, 14
Holding Hands, 43
Home Wreckers, The, 210
Honey Bear, 61
Hot Chocolate, 200
Hot Hippo, 42
Hot Hippo (video), 45
House at Pooh Corner, The, 204
House Crickets, 106
House for Hermit Crab, A, 170
House Mouse, The, 101
How Do I Put It On?, 175
How Giraffe Got Such a Long Neck and Why Rhino Is So Grumpy, 42
How Many Bugs in a Box?, 71
How Much Is That Doggie in the Window?, 211
How to Fold a Paper Crane (video), 51, 54
How to Make an Apple Pie and See the World, 188
Howjadoo (recording), 67, 192
Humming Birds, 52
Humpty Dumpty, 26, 159
Hungry Morning, 52
Hungry Wolf, The, 22
Hunky Dory Ate It, 186
Hurry, Hurry, Mary Dear, 204
Hurry, Hurry, Mary Dear and Other Nonsense Poems, 179, 204
Hurt No Living Thing, 75
Hushabye My Darling, 92
Hypnotized, 146

I Am a Pizza, 189
I Am a Snowman, 202–3
I Am Falling Off a Mountain, 163
I Am Running in a Circle, 163
I Can Do Something I Bet You Can't Do, 110
I Can Put My Clothes On by Myself, 179

I Can Put My Socks On, 179
I Can Take a Bath, 66
I Did a Nutty Somersault, 163
I Don't Wanna Go to School, 157
I Drive My Mommy Crazy, 145
I Eat My Peas with Honey, 16
I Found a Four-Leaf Clover, 163
I Had a Rooster, 32
I Had an Old Coat, 179
I Hate My Name, 121
I Hold My Fingers Like a Fish, 173
I Know an Old Lady Who Swallowed a Fly, 16
I Know an Old Lady Who Swallowed a Pie, 184
I Like to Be Cold and Wet, 205
I Love Mud, 67
I Love You, I Love You, 183
I Should Have Stayed in Bed Today, 163
I Speak, I Say, I Talk, 110
I Wanna Be a Dog, 212
I Want a Pet Porcupine, Mother, 43
I Want You to Meet, 75
I Wouldn't, 101
Ice Cream Store, The, 33, 121, 172
If a Grizzly Bear Had Feathers, 61
If I Were in Charge of the World, 26, 144, 212
If Walt Whitman Had Written Humpty Dumpty, 26
If We Didn't Have Birthdays, 16
If You Ever Meet a Whale, 169
If You Give a Mouse a Cookie, 99
If You Give a Mouse a Cookie (video), 103
If You Love a Hippopotamus, 37
If Your Clothes Have Any Red, 177–8
If You're Happy and You Know It, 16

If You're No Good at Cooking, 188
Iktomi and the Boulder, 156
I'm a Dirty Kid, 63
I'm a Little Teapot, 17
I'm a Little Toad, 85–6
I'm Being Swallowed by a Boa Constrictor, 85
I'm Much Too Tired to Play Tonight, 92
Imagine That (recording), 121
Improvise with Eric Nagler (recording), 145
In Daddy's Arms, I Am Tall, 136
In Search of Cinderella, 26
Incredibly Spreadable (recording), 110
Insects Are My Life, 71
Invitation, 4
Ira Sleeps Over (video), 94
Is It Time?, 65
Is Your Mama a Llama?, 140
It's My Family, 137
It's the Truth (recording), 61
It's Time to Go to Bed, 93
It's Too Noisy, 110
I've Got a Dog, 208
I've Got a Dog and His Name Is Cat, 212
I've Got a Yo-Yo (recording), 43, 52, 157, 164

Jack and Jill, 159
Jack Be Nimble, 159
Jazzy Three Bears, 26
Jelly, Jelly, in My Belly, 186–7
Jenny Jenkins, 175
Jeremy Kooloo, 98
Jeremy's Muffler, 204
Jesse Bear, What Will You Wear?, 176
Jim Hensen: A Sesame Street Celebration (recording), 63
Joe's First Video, 143, 146
John Jacob Jingleheimer Schmidt, 121
Joke, The, 148

Jolly Postman and Other People's Letters, The, 21, 22
Josephina Hates Her Name, 120
Jump Children (recording), 56, 61, 93, 129
Just Enough to Make a Story, 130
Just Grandma and Me, 141
Just Like Daddy, 136

Keep a Poem in Your Pocket, 91
Kidding Around (recording), 14
Kids in Motion (recording), 157
Kids Pick the Funniest Poems, 74, 189
Kids Songs 2 (recording), 65, 164
King Bidgood's in the Bathtub, 64
King Bidgood's in the Bathtub (video), 68
King of the Birds, The, 52
Kiss for Little Bear, A, 15
Kiwi, 52
Klunge Maker, The, 2, 168–9

Lamb Chop's Sing-Along, Play-Along (recording), 111
Last Cry of the Damp Fly, The, 75
Late Last Night, 127
Late Last Night (recording), 164
Lazy Lion, 196
Leading Kids to Books through Magic, 148
Let's Give Kitty a Bath (video), 68, 103
Let's Go Froggy, 136
Let's Play in the Snow, 205
Letter from Goldilocks, 21
Letter from Red Riding Hood, 22
Light in the Attic, A, 26, 129
Lion, 196

Lisa Lee Elizabeth, 121
Little Birds, The, 47
Little Bunny Foo Foo, 101
Little Donkey, Close Your Eyes, 92
Little Ducklings, The, 34–5
Little Girl Named Riding Hood, A, 180–1
Little Mo, 59
Little Mouse, the Red Ripe Strawberry, and the Big Hungry Bear, The, 97
Little Peep, 30
Little Rap Riding Hood, 22
Little Red Riding Hood: A Newfangled Prairie Tale, 25
Little Spider, 76
Little Tricker the Squirrel Meets Big Double the Bear, 156
Little White Duck, The (recording), 101
Long Johns, 179
Lost Cat, 129
Louella Mae, She's Run Away, 33
Love Letters, 136
Lunch, 185
Lunch Box, 184

McElligot's Pool, 172
Madalina Catalina, 121
maggie and milly and molly and may, 121
Magic Boots, The, 128
Mail Myself to You (recording), 34
Mailbox Poem, The, 144
Mainly Mother Goose (recording), 73, 101
Make a Snow Family, 203
Make Believe (recording), 15
Make Way for Ducklings, 12
Make Way for Ducklings (video), 18
Mama Don't Allow (video), 112
Mama Said, 145–6
Man Who Didn't Wash His Dishes, The, 15

Martha Speaks, 210
Martha Speaks (video), 214
Marvelous Toy, The, 132–3
Mary Had a Little Lamb, 26
Mary Had a Stick of Gum, 26
Maxie and the Taxi, 160
Meatballs and Spaghetti, 189
Melinda Mae, 172
Mice, 96
Mice Are Nice, 101
Mice Squeak, We Speak, 110
Midnight Snowman, 202
Mike Mulligan and His Steam Shovel, 15
Mike Mulligan and His Steam Shovel (video), 18
Millions of Cats, 12–13
Milton, the Early Riser, 60
Miss Bindergarten Gets Ready for Kindergarten, 117
Miss Mary Mack, 180
Mistress Pat, 129
Mitten, The, 201
Mitten, The, 201, 205
Mitten Song, The, 204
Mitten Tree, The, 203
Mom Is Wow!, 140
Monkey Face, 140
Monsters' Holiday (recording), 121, 164
Moonstruck, 93
Moose Music, 110
More It Snows, The, 204
More Surprises, 196
Mosquito, The, 72
Mother Earth (recording), 189
Mother's Day, 140
Mother's Day Sandwich, The, 144
Mouse Count, 101
Mouse Paint, 98
Mouse TV, 100
Mouthsounds, 105, 106
Mr. Putter and Tabby Walk the Dog, 212
Mrs. Piggle Wiggle's Won't-Take-a-Bath-Cure, 63
Mrs. Toggle's Zipper, 175
Mud Puddle, 66

Muddy Puddle, The, 67
Musical Max, 110
My Aunt Came Back, 141–2
My Best Shoes, 128
My Brother Eats Bugs, 70
My Brown Bear Barney, 57
My Camera: At the Aquarium, 168
My Cats Nick and Nora, 100
My Dad, 137
My Dog He Is an Ugly Dog, 212
My Dog's Bigger Than Your Dog, 208
My Hat Has Three Corners, 125
My Kitten's Mittens, 177, 180
My Life with the Wave, 171
My Mom and Dad Make Me Laugh, 178
My Mother Doesn't Want a Dog, 212
My Mother Ran Away Today, 145
My New and Squeaky Shoes, 126
My Opinion, 75
My Teddy Bear, 61
My Turtle, 80–1
My Uncle, 136

Name Game, The, 114
Naming the Cat, 120
Napping House, The, 89
Napping House, The (video), 94
Nathaniel Willy, Scared Silly, 89
Naughty Soap Song, 64
Never Take a Pig to Lunch, 75
New Adventures of Mother Goose, The, 159
New Jacket, 179
New Kid on the Block, The, 67, 163, 189, 212
New Shoes for Silvia, 128
New Treasury of Children's Poetry, A, 16, 204
New Wheels on the Bus, The, 24
Newts, Salamanders and Frogs, 85

Night Bear, 61
Night Driving, 136
Night I Followed the Dog, The, 212
Night the Froggies Flew, The, 78
Night Warning, 93
Nine Black Cats, 97
Noise Day, 110
Noisy Nora (video), 112
Northern Lullaby, 92

Oats and Beans and Barley Grow, 30–1
Octopus, 168
Octopus Hug, 132
Officer Buckle and Gloria (video), 165
Oh, Have You Heard, 156
Oh, Please Take Me Fishing, 172
Oh, Woe Ith Me, 160
Old Black Fly, 74
Old Dog, New Tricks (recording), 212
Old John Muddlecombe, 130
Old MacDonald, 29
Old MacDonald Had a Farm, 33
Old Mother Hubbard, 20
Old Woman, The, 68
On the Funny Farm, 34
On the Road of Stars: Native American Night Poems and Sleep Charms, 93
On the Trail (recording), 205
On Top of Spaghetti, 14
Once I Saw Three Goats, 179
Once upon a Rhyme, 43, 179
One Elephant (recording), 75
One Elephant Went Out to Play, 44–5
One Shoe Bear, 61
1-2-3 for Kids (recording), 14, 67, 85, 177
Oops, 164
Open Them, Shut Them, 16–17
Origami Birds, 51

Oscar, Bingo and Buddies (recording), 61
Other Side of the Door, The, 61, 121, 172
Otto the Hippo, 44
Over in the Meadow (video), 198
Owl Moon, 134
Owl Moon, 134–5
Owl Moon (video), 138

Pancake, The, 190
Panther, The, 197
Paper Bag Princess, The, 25
Paper Crane, The, 51
Paper Crane, The (video), 54
Paper Pandas and Jumping Frogs, 51
Parade, The, 75
Parents in the Pigpen, Pigs in the Tub, 30
Pass the Fritters Critters, 188
Peace at Last, 90, 107
Peanut, The, 165
Peck Slither and Slide, 195
Peek-a-Boo (recording), 179
Peeping Beauty (video), 54
People Upstairs, The, 16
Perfect Father's Day, A, 136
Peter, Paul and Mommy, Too (recording), 16, 85
Peter Ping and Patrick Pong, 121
Pick Up Your Room, 144
Pickety Fence, The, 110
Piggy in the Puddle, The (video), 68
Piggyback Planet (recording), 75
Pizza the Size of the Sun, A, 136, 163, 172
Place in the Choir, A, 192
Playing Favorites (recording), 26
Plenty of Room, 157
Poem for a Pickle, A, 212
Poem Stew, 26
Poems for Grandmothers, 144

Poems for the Very Young, 61, 96, 179, 188
Poems of A. Nonny Mouse, 26, 85, 110, 212
Polka Dots, Checks and Stripes, 179
Pondlarker, 78–9
Poppy the Panda, 59
Porcupine Named Fluffy, A, 38, 120
Porridge, 56–7
Prayer of the Little Duck, The, 34
Principal's New Clothes, The, 25
Puppies and Kittens, 213–14
Puppies, Dogs, and Blue Northers: Reflections on Being Raised by a Pack of Sled Dogs, 210
Puppy and the Cat, The, 208–9
Puppy Chased the Sunbeam, The, 212
Pure Imagination (recording), 15, 137, 179
Purple Coat, The (video), 181
Purple Cow, The, 16
Put Your Finger in the Air, 16
Put Your Thumbs in the Air, 159–60

Quack! Said the Billy Goat, 34
Queen of Eene, The, 129
Quiet Mother and the Noisy Little Boy, The, 144
Quiet Mouse, The, 98

Raffi in Concert with the Rise and Shine Band (recording), 49
Rags, 213
Rainbow Fish, The, 171
Raindrops, 75
Rainhat, The, 130
Random House Book of Poetry for Children, The, 16, 81, 85, 96, 121, 204

Rattlesnake Meat, 189
*Read-Aloud Rhymes for the Very
  Young,* 16, 43, 52, 61, 67, 75,
  85, 101, 110, 189, 212
Read This with Gestures, 200
*Ready . . . Set . . . Read—and
  Laugh,* 144
Recipe for a Hippopotamus
  Sandwich, 39
Red Lace, Yellow Lace, 127
Red Riding Hood (video), 27
Rescue of Aunt Pansy, The, 100
Rhinoceros, The, 43
Rise and Shine (recording), 49,
  111
Rock-a-Bye Baby, 94
Rock and Roll Dog, 213
Rock 'n' Roll Teddy Bear
  (recording), 212
Rosenshontz Tickles You
  (recording), 44, 157
Rosie's Walk (video), 35
Round of Applause, A, 215
Round Robin, 51
Rover, 212
Royal Nap, The, 109
Rubber Blubber Whale, 67
Rubber Duckie, 63
Rumble in the Jungle, 195
Rumpelstiltskin, 120
Runaway Bunny, The, 143

*Sad Underwear and Other
  Complications,* 26, 156
Sailor Went to Sea, A, 167
Sand Cake, 60
Saturday Sancocho, 188
Sea, The, 167
Sea Shell, The, 173
Seven Blind Mice, 39
Shake It All About (recording),
  14, 16
*Shake It to the One That You
  Love the Best: Play Songs and
  Lullabies from Black Musical
  Traditions* (recording), 66
Shakin' a Tailfeather (record-
  ing), 114

Share It (recording), 56, 61, 93
Sheep in a Jeep, 160
Sheep Out to Eat, 163
*Sheep, Sheep, Sheep, Help Me
  Fall Asleep,* 92
She'll Be Comin' Round the
  Mountain, 16
*Side by Side: Poems to Read
  Together,* 43, 110
Silly Names for My Toes, 118
Silly Sally, 117
Sillytime Magic (recording),
  114
Simply Singable (recording),
  129
Sing a Song of Popcorn, 75
Sing a Song of Seasons (record-
  ing), 205
Sing A to Z (recording), 210
Sing Along Stew (recording), 75
*Singable Songs for the Very
  Young* (recording), 80
Singing in the Tub, 67
Singing 'n' Swinging (record-
  ing), 179
Sitting Down to Eat, 196
Six Crows, 48
Skateboard, 143
Skiing, 204
Skunk Song, The, 13
Sky Is Full of Song, The, 52
Sleep, Sleep, 93
Sleepy Fingers, 91
Slugs at Sea (recording), 52,
  167
Smile for Auntie (video), 146
Smorgasbord (recording), 34
Sneakers, 129
Snip, Snip . . . Snow!, 200
Snow Dance, 204
Snow Song, 205
Snowballs, 200, 203
Snowballs, 204
Snowchild, The, 204
Snowy Day, The (video), 206
So Cold Outside, 205
*Soap! Soap! Soap! Don't Forget
  the Soap!,* 162
Sody Salleratus, 152–5

Some of These Stories, 5
Some Things Don't Make Any
   Sense at All, 144
Somebody and the Three Blairs,
   21
Someday Someone Will Bet
   That You Can't Name All
   Fifty States, 156
Something Big Has Been Here,
   43, 92, 144, 163
Something in My Shoe, 111
Something's Coming!, 92
Song and Dance Man, 135
Song to Straighten a Bad
   Dream, 93
Songs from Dreamland, 93
Sounds from A to Z, 105
Soup, 200
Sparrow, 52
Spence Makes Circles, 142
Spider on the Floor, 72–3
Spin a Soft Black Song, 67
Splish Splash: Bath Time Fun
   (recording), 63
Squirrel's Got a Bushy Tail,
   198
"Stand Back," Said the
   Elephant, "I'm Going to
   Sneeze," 43
Star Light, Star Bright, 25
Stardreamer (recording), 61, 91
Sticky Bubblegum, 162
Still as a Star: A Book of
   Nighttime Poems, 93
Stinky Feet, 129
Stocking and Shirt, 179
Stomache Surprise, 189
Stone Soup, 189
Stone Soup, 15
Stone Soup (video), 18
Stories and Songs for Little
   Children (recording), 85
Story about Ping, The (video),
   54
Story of Ferdinand, The, 15
Strega Nona, 163
Strega Nona (video), 165
Super-Duper Peanut Butter and
   Jelly Sandwich, The, 184–5

Super Mom, 145
Surprises, 61, 163
Susie and the Alligator, 85
Swimmy, 171

Tacky the Penguin, 40
Tailor and the Mouse, The,
   101
Talking Like the Rain: A First
   Book of Poems, 101
Teacher's Favorites (recording),
   157, 179
Teddy Bear Rap, 59–60
Teddy Bear's Greatest Hits
   (recording), 26, 56
Teddy Bear's Picnic, 56
Tell Me a Story, Mama, 144
10 Carrot Diamond (record-
   ing), 189
Ten Dogs in the Window, 211
Ten Galloping Horses,
   111–12
Ten Kinds, 121
There Was a Small Dog Named
   Maggie, 212
There Was an Old Lady Who
   Lived in a Shoe, 124
There's a Hippo in My Tub, 67
There's a Hole in the Bottom of
   the Sea, 170–1
There's Music in a Hammer,
   100, 110
These Are the Questions, 157
Thing That Bothered Farmer
   Brown, The, 74
Things to Do if You Are a Star,
   90
This Is My Turtle, 86
This Is the Bear, 60
This Is the Hat, 128
This Is the Way We Dress
   Ourselves, 176
This Little Cow, 35
This Little Song, 111
This Quiet Lady, 144
This Song Is for the Birds, 47
Thomas' Snowsuit, 178
Three Cheers for Tacky, 52

Three Cool Kids, 25
Three Craw, 48–9
Three Hat Day, A (video), 130
Three Little Kittens, 101
Three Little Pigs, The (video), 27
Three Little Pigs Blues, The, 26
Three Little Smelly Skunks, 194–5
Three Little Snowmen, 201–2
Three Stories You Can Read to Your Dog, 208
Three Wolves and the Big Bad Pig, The, 20
Thunder Cake, 140
Tiger, 197
Tikki Tikki Tembo, 115
Tikki Tikki Tembo (video), 122
Time to Sleep, 93
To Bathe a Boa, 66
Toll Bridge Troll, The, 148
Tom Tigercat, 197
Tomie DePaola's Book of Poems, 110
Tommy, Don't Lick That Pipe, 200
Tommy Thumbs, 117
Tony Chestnut, 118–19
Too Many Daves, 116
Too Quiet for These Old Bones, 106
Tops and Bottoms, 156
Tops and Bottoms (video), 157
Tortoise and the Hare, The, 84
Tot Rock (recording), 145, 197
Travel Song Sing Alongs (recording), 93
Tricking, 156
Trio of Myopic Rodents, A, 20
Trips, 67
True Story of the Three Little Pigs, The, 25
Tucking-In Song, 93
Tuesday, 78
Turtle in July, 52
Twinkle, Twinkle, Little Star, 90–1
Two Fat Sausages, 186
Two Fine Grandpas, 138

Two Little Black Birds, 26–7
Two of Everything, 159
Two Sad, 189
Two Skunks, 194
Two Terrible Frights, 88–9
Tying My Shoe, 127

Uh-Oh (recording), 34, 159
Unbearable Bears (recording), 56, 61, 93
Uncle Dave's Car, 136
Underwear, 179
Use Your Own Two Feet, 129

Very Busy Spider, The, 74
Very Hungry Caterpillar, The, 74, 185
Very Lonely Firefly, The, 72
Very Quiet Cricket, The, 74, 106

Waiters, 156
Wake Up, Wake Up, 90
Wally's Rhyme, 121
Walter's Tail, 211
Waltzing with Bears, 61
Water-Go-Round, The, 172
Watermelon, 189
Wave Goodbye, 6
Way Down South, 45
Way They Scrub, The, 67
We All Live Together, Vol. 1 (recording), 16, 66, 117
We All Live Together, Vol. 4 (recording), 210
We Will Rock You, 105
We Will, We Will Read Books!, 105–6
Wee Sing (recording), 101, 164
Wee Sing Fun 'n' Folk (recording), 61
Wee Sing Silly Songs (recording), 20, 30
We're Going on a Bear Hunt, 60
We're Going to Kentucky, 108–9

We've All Got Stories (recording), 29
What Could a Hippopotamus Be?, 39
What Does Your Mama Do?, 145
What Fun to Be a Hippopotamus, 43
What You Do Is Easy, What I Do Is Hard, 196
What You Gonna Wear?, 175
When a Jolly Young Fisher, 167
When Bluebell Sang, 33
When I Found a Mouse in My Stew, 99
When It Comes to Bugs, 74
When Johnny Comes Marching Home, 47
When My Shoes Are Loose, 128
When the Cows Get Up in the Morning, 29
When the Dark Comes Dancing: A Bedtime Poetry Book, 92
When the Rooster Crowed, 33
When Tillie Ate the Chili, 189
Where Do My Sneakers Go at Night? (recording), 121, 137
Where Does It Go?, 178
Where Is Thumbkin?, 13
Where the Sidewalk Ends, 5, 34, 52, 156, 172
Where's My Pajamas, 93
Where's My Teddy?, 60
Whiskers and Rhymes, 129
Who to Pet and Who Not to Pet, 163
Who Took the Farmer's Hat?, 128
Who Wants a Cheap Rhinoceros?, 43
Whole Bed, 89
Whoops Johnny, 151

Who's in Rabbit's House?, 38, 155
Who's in Rabbit's House? (video), 157
Whose Hat?, 125
Whose Shoe?, 126
Why Is It?, 175
Why Mosquitoes Buzz in People's Ears (video), 198
Why It's Hard to Be Romantic If You're an Octopus, 172
Willoughby Wallaby Woo, 114
Winter Clothes, 204
Winter Poems, 204
Wintersongs (recording), 200
Wise Old Owl, A, 54
Wolf's Chicken Stew, The, 183
Wombat Stew, 194
Woody's 20 Grow Big Songs (recording), 16

Yankee Doodle, 71, 124
Yellow Butter, 189
Yellow Butter, Purple Jelly, Red Jam, Black Bread, 43, 85, 156, 172, 189, 197
You Be Good and I'll Be Night, 93
You Be Saucer, I'll Be Cup, 93
You Can't Catch Me!, 74
You Can't Make a Turtle Come Out, 81
You're My Turtle, You're My Dove, 133
You've No Need to Light a Night Light, 88
Yucka Drucka Droni, 121

Zag Zig (recording), 157
Zomo the Rabbit, 151
Zooful of Animals, A, 101

Rob Reid is the author of *Children's Jukebox: A Subject Guide to Musical Recordings and Programming Ideas for Songsters Ages One to Twelve* (ALA, 1995) and the picture book *Wave Goodbye* (Lee and Low, 1996). He worked as a children's librarian for fourteen years and now teaches full-time at the University of Wisconsin–Eau Claire. He drives a minivan he calls "Clifford the Big Red Van."